11/08

HDTV and the Transition to Digital Broadcasting

HDTV and the Transition to Digital Broadcasting

Understanding New Television Technologies

Philip J. Cianci

AMSTERDAM • BOSTON • HEIDELBERG • LONDON
NEW YORK • OXFORD • PARIS • SAN DIEGO
SAN FRANCISCO • SINGAPORE • SYDNEY • TOKYO

Focal Press Is an Imprint of Elsevier

ELSEVIER

Acquisitions Editor:	Angelina Ward
Publishing Services Manager:	George Morrison
Project Manager:	Kathryn Liston
Assistant Editor:	Doug Shults
Development Editor:	Beth Millett
Marketing Manager:	Christine Degon Veroulis
Cover Design:	Eric Decicco

Focal Press is an imprint of Elsevier
30 Corporate Drive, Suite 400, Burlington, MA 01803, USA
Linacre House, Jordan Hill, Oxford OX2 8DP, UK

∞ Recognizing the importance of preserving what has been written, Elsevier prints its
books on acid-free paper whenever possible.

Library of Congress Cataloging-in-Publication Data
Application submitted

British Library Cataloguing-in-Publication Data
A catalogue record for this book is available from the British Library.

ISBN 13: 978-0-240-80904-5
ISBN 10: 0-240-80904-1

For information on all Focal Press publications
visit our website at www.books.elsevier.com

07 08 09 10 11   10 9 8 7 6 5 4 3 2 1

Printed in the United States of America

Working together to grow
libraries in developing countries

www.elsevier.com | www.bookaid.org | www.sabre.org

ELSEVIER   BOOK AID International   Sabre Foundation

Contents

*This book is dedicated to
the memory of my father...*

Acknowledgements

Some material in this book has previously appeared in *Broadcast Engineering* magazine articles and the magazine's *Transition to Digital* e-Newsletters. That material is used herein with permission of Prism Media, 2006. I owe that opportunity and my thanks to Brad Dick, editorial director, who took a chance on an unpublished writer.

Thank you to the Advanced Television Systems Committee for permission to use numerous drawings from their suite of standards documents. The most recent versions can be found at www.atsc.org. The Society of Motion Picture and Television Engineers www.smpte.org and the AAF Association www.aafassociation.org have also graciously allowed use of drawings from their documents.

Historical material is derived from my recollections that have been contributed to the Smithsonian Institution, final resting place of the Grand Alliance prototype. I'd like to thank Dr. Bernard Finn, now retired, from the Smithsonian Institution, for allowing me to participate in the establishment of an HDTV archive.

Chapter 2 is actually a collaborative effort. Aldo Cugnini added much of the audio history and touched up other sections. Glenn Reitmeier reviewed the entire chapter and made many useful observations. Thanks to all. To comment about this chapter, visit www.HDTVarchiveproject.com.

Without the opportunity offered to me by Dr. Rich Prodan to join Philips Laboratories in 1984, I never would have caught the first wave of HD research and development. Carlo Basile, Aldo Cugnini, Dave Bryan, Mikhael Tsinberg, Charlie Rhodes and all the others I worked with and for during my 17 years there have contributed to my career in TV in one way or another.

If Jim Scott and Alex Best had never taken a chance and brought me on board as the overnight engineer at AT&T Digital Media Center, 17 Battery Place, New York City, I might not have made the leap into the operations side of the TV business.

When it was 5 a.m. and the sun was rising, casting red rays that silhouetted the Statue of Liberty, in my wildest dreams I couldn't have imagined that Bob Regina would hire me to work at ESPN just as the all-HD Digital Center project was hitting its stride.

I owe a great deal of thanks to Ted Szypulski, a senior director at ESPN for the chance to author presentations for SMPTE's New York chapter, STE in California, IBC and for an NAB paper as well.

At Focal Press, Angelina Ward turned down my original proposal but offered this instead. I am grateful for this opportunity and for her guidance and support. Without Beth Millett, who spent uncounted hours getting this work into a presentable form, the technical level of this work may have been beyond the comprehension of the intended reader. I owe her my thanks for a great team effort.

My career in technology has been influenced by family members. When I was very young, the magic of visiting my cousin Ronald Cianci, who due to an accident, was confined to wheel chair, and seeing the map of the world and his HAM radio contacts was amazing. My late Uncle Vincent Tedone's career at IBM in Poughkeepsie inspired me to take a gamble on a better life when Honeywell Medical offered me a test technician position. And my late ex-father-in-law, Robert Arculeo, helped me adjust to big time R&D by relating many of his experiences during a career at IBM's Watson Research Center.

But my start in TV, building cat-whisker radios and mastering the use of a Simpson meter, was primarily due to my late father, Phil Cianci, a WWII radio technician. This broadcasting career began on the roof of a three story apartment building in Harrison, NY, where we ceremoniously set-up a high gain antenna, on certain Sundays in the fall of 1963, pointed it toward New Haven and watched very NY Football Giants blacked-out home game.

And then there's my virtual other half, Marcie, my captive audience, who had no choice but to listen to my unceasing lectures about broadcast engineering. To her I give my undying love and affection …

Drawing Sources

ATSC

- A/52B: Digital Audio Compression (AC-3) (E-AC-3) Standard, Rev. B

- A/53E: ATSC Digital Television Standard, Revision E with Amendments No. 1 and No. 2

- A/54A: Guide to the Use of the ATSC Digital Television Standard

- A/65C: Program and System Information Protocol for Terrestrial Broadcast and Cable, Revision C, with Amendment No. 1

- A/69: Program and System Information Protocol Implementation Guidelines for Broadcasters

- A/100: DTV Application Software Environment – Level 1 (DASE-1)

SMPTE

- Joint EBU/SMPTE Task Force for Harmonized Standards for the Exchange of Program Material as Bit Streams
  - First Report: User Requirements – April 1997
  - Final Report: Analyses and Results – July 1998

- EG 41-2004: Material Exchange Format (MXF) Engineering Guideline

- SMPTE 260M-1999: for Television – Digital Representation and Bit-Parallel Interface – 1125/60 High-Definition Production System

AAF Association

Understanding AAF – A Powerpoint presentation, presented as part of the Digital Video Production Workshop at NAB 2000

Author Biography

Philip J. Cianci joined Philips Laboratories, Briarcliff Manor, New York, as a research assistant in 1984 and worked on HDTV prototype systems including the Grand Alliance prototype MPEG-2 Video Decoder. He participated in the NIST ATP Digital Studio Project and managed the commissioning of a Video Simulation Infrastructure, a precursor of a server-based HDTV digital broadcast operations center.

Working overnights at AT&T Digital Media Center in lower Manhattan during 2002 facilitated his initiation to the broadcast operations side of the TV business.

Mr. Cianci was a first-hand witness to HDTV history. Beginning in 2003, he was at ESPN during the construction, commissioning and opening night of the all-HD Digital Center. While there, he co-authored presentations for IBC, NAB and other industry events.

Mr. Cianci is editor of Broadcast Engineering Magazine's *Transition to Digital* e-newsletter. Since 2002, he has been working with the Smithsonian Institution to build an HDTV archive of first-person accounts and artifacts from the R&D, standards setting, infrastructure deployment and program broadcasting phases of HDTV.

When not writing, Cianci keeps his creative energies flowing as both an experimental painter and composer. He relaxes by enjoying a round of golf and an evening of ballroom dancing.

Introduction

HDTV has been described as a technology looking for a business model. As the effort to develop HDTV began, many questioned not only its technical feasibility but its business viability as well. Once the standard was adopted, broadcasters were reluctant to incur the expense to convert to a digital production and transmission infrastructure. The end of the transition to digital broadcasting is in sight. In February 2009, analog over-the-air television ceases to exist in the U.S.

It may be human nature to trivialize a technology that has become commoditized. It may be human nature to underestimate the complexity of something one does not understand. Yes fools rush in where angels fear to tread. This approach is a fatal attitude at this crucial moment of media industry disruption. Digital television technology is not simple.

Who Should Read this Book

This book is intended for the intelligent, inquisitive broadcast professional who desires to understand the technologies that HDTV and the transition to DTV are built upon. As with many complex technologies, the development of HDTV was not just about building a better mousetrap.

Written for executives, managers and non-technical broadcast personnel, a reader can absorb basic DTV concepts and terminology in a quick read. Yet enough technical detail is presented so that those interested in a deeper understanding of technology and standards important to DTV can be acquired. This also makes this book a good starting point for IT and creative professionals, application authors and anyone who desires to get the "BIG PICTURE" of DTV Technology.

Executive Summary

The broadcasting business today is in the midst of a disruptive technology revolution. At a rapidly increasing rate, new, relevant technologies are being introduced, and technical standards are being established.

Digital broadcasting is fundamentally different from its analog predecessor. Besides the transmission of perfect digital audio and video, DTV has ushered in a new content transport paradigm. Programs that were delivered as a single analog composite signal now arrive at a DTV receiver as separate audio, video and data packets with assembly instructions.

This book follows two underlying precepts. The first is to describe the differences between analog NTSC technology and digital broadcasting technologies. The second is to supply enough information for the non-technical broadcast professional to ask the right questions in order to understand the underlying engineering principles necessary to successfully transition their organizations to HDTV and digital broadcasting.

Transition to Digital

Viewer relationship management, facilitating enhanced, interactive and personalized features, will aid broadcasters in developing brand awareness and loyalty. TV will move from a mass media to a one-to-one personalized experience.

As the audience of content consumers votes with its attention, time and dollars, the marketplace will determine (as always) what media business models will succeed in the DTV era.

This book covers some of the esoteric mysteries that enable HD and DTV to be commoditized. Based on human perception and digital technology, the engineering effort to bring this life-like sensory experience to the communication domain stands as a high point in the application of technology to increase understanding among the people and nations of the world.

Digital broadcasting was born in the U.S. in 1996 with the adoption of a terrestrial DTV standard, took its first steps in 1998 HDTV broadcasts, and survived its adolescence in the early 2000s with the conversion and construction of digital production infrastructures. Digital broadcasting will come of age with the shutdown of analog NTSC broadcasting in 2009.

Few thought the transition to digital broadcasting would be easy, and fewer had any idea that it would be this hard and take this long. But it will ultimately be successful beyond all expectations.

1 The Dawn of HDTV and Digital Television

Walk around a consumer electronics store and look at all the different kinds of high definition televisions. Flat-panel LCDs, plasma displays, DLP and LCoS Projection TVs abound, while receivers with cathode ray tube (CRT) displays are becoming increasingly scarce.

Receiver labels proclaim "HDTV-ready," "built-in ATSC decoder," and "EDTV." Display specifications tout resolutions of 1366 × 1080, 1024 × 720 and formats of 1080i, 720p or 1080p. How many different kinds of HDTV are there? What does it all mean?

As difficult as it is for the consumer, it is significantly worse for television professionals. Veteran broadcast engineers have to learn a new kind of television, one based predominantly on digital technologies. Each digital subsystem of a broadcast infrastructure is now an area of expertise that technology professionals have spent a lifetime pursuing competence in.

It may be even more of a challenge for experienced broadcast industry professionals—who don't have engineering or computer science degrees—to understand the obscure jargon and technical complexity of modern digital broadcast systems. In the past, operational experience was usually sufficient to specify production systems. This first-hand knowledge enabled a production or operational oriented viewpoint to guide the underlying infrastructure design and facilitated the inclusion of required capabilities and desired features.

Analog broadcast systems consisted of mostly stand-alone components interconnected by real-time audio and video signals. When something went wrong, "divide and conquer" trouble-shooting techniques could be used to quickly isolate the problem and take corrective action.

All this has changed. Digital broadcasting, and its merging of broadcast engineering and information technology, has created a networked environment where every piece of equipment is interconnected.

Analog and Digital TV Compared

In analog television systems, audio and video are transmitted as one complete "composite" signal. But with digital TV, audio and video are separately processed and transmitted as discrete packets. When processing streams of digital content, there must be a way to differentiate groups of bits and bytes into program elements.

The transmission must include information that identifies which bits are video and which are audio. Assembly instructions for these components are also included in the transmission, so the digital television receiver knows how to combine the audio and video pieces into a complete program for presentation. Other data provides information for the electronic program guide, closed captions and other features.

All this is enabled by metadata, data that is not the actual audio or video content of a program but provides organizational and descriptive information which is now just as important as audio or video. Metadata is discussed in greater depth in Chapter 5.

Analog versus digital quality

Until the advent of high quality digital encoding techniques, analog audio and video was considered more aesthetically pleasing than a digital representation of the same content. So when CD technology was invented, many audiophiles argued that it was inferior to analog sound recording because the act of digitizing the audio creates steps or discrete units that approximately represent the sound, whereas sound in nature, and when represented in analog form, is a smooth, continuous wave. But digitization of sound works because these steps are so small that the auditory system perceives the sound as continuous.

An important advantage of digitization is noise immunity. For example, if electronic noise contaminates an analog audio signal, the fidelity of the sound is diminished and eventually too much noise becomes annoying. With digitized sound, a "1' is a one and a "0" is a zero, well past the annoying analog noise threshold. In other words, the same amount of noise that makes an analog signal unpleasant has no effect at all on a digital representation of the same sound.

Perception is at the core of digital processing of visual and aural information. Reduction of audio and video data is facilitated by an understanding of the physiology, neurology and psychology of sensory stimulation. Psychovisual and psychoaural algorithmic models are applied to audio and video source material to reduce the amount of data necessary for apparent perfect fidelity. In this way, unperceived sensory information is discarded.

Data compression techniques, when properly applied to digitized audio and video, permit the transfer of high quality content over broadcast facility production networks and transmission channels. In the consumer environment, compressed media enables content transfer and consumption in a digital home media network. The explosion of MP3 audio and the rapid emergence of video downloads over the Internet is an example of how compression is an enabling technology for new content distribution business models.

Analog Television

In the U.S., the National Television System Committee (NTSC) black-and-white television standard was established in 1940. Regular over the air (OTA) broadcasts began on July 1, 1941. The aspect ratio of the display was set at 4:3 (horizontal by vertical), with 525 lines of vertical resolution, about 480 of which are active and display an image 30 times per second. In the horizontal direction, cathode ray tube technology facilitated a continuous trace and an absence of discrete picture elements, resulting in the intensity of portions of the line being varied.

In 1953, National Television Systems Committee II (NTSC II) defined the color television broadcasting technical standard. Color television broadcasts had to be compatible with NTSC I so black-and-white sets could receive and properly decode an NTSC II signal. The frame rate was altered to yield about 29.97 fps to avoid color dot-crawl effects and audio distortion.

TV engineering developed a numerical measure of the equivalent number of picture elements ("pixels") for analog displays. However, the bandwidth of the NTSC signal reduces the number of vertical resolution elements and the number of horizontal resolution elements. The result is that an analog NTSC 4:3 display can be said to have a resolution of 340 $\times$ 330 pixels. In the computer display world this is about the same as the CGA display mode.

One must be careful not to confuse the number of lines and pixels on a display with the resolution of the display. For example, if lines of alternating white and black make up the vertical dimension of a 100-line display, then the ability to resolve visual information is half that number. Resolution is a measure of the smallest detail that can be presented, i.e., 50 pairs of alternating black and white lines. It is influenced by the audio and video signal processing chain.

Digital Television

Digital television, or DTV, presents a conceptual shift for creation production, distribution and consumption of television programs. With the advent of digital cameras, digital tape machines, compression, microprocessors, computer networks, packetized data transport and digital modulation, DTV is the consummation of communications engineering, computer science and information technologies developed in the twentieth century. In effect, DTV is a bit pipe into a receiving device. In addition to audio and video, this allows data delivery features and applications.

Digital data compression techniques, combined with error correction, facilitate "squeezing" a picture and sound into a standard broadcast channel. Although, in principle, many levels of DTV resolution are available, high definition (HD) and standard definition (SD) are the two general descriptions of the level of visual detail. HDTV, when viewed on a display that supports full resolution and adequate bit rates, is close enough to reality to provide an experience of immersion, particularly if multi-channel surround sound is included in the broadcast. SDTV is similar to analog television as seen in a broadcast studio but the digital signal processing provides a superior picture in the home compared to any deliverable via NTSC.

Today, digital broadcasters have the option to "multicast." That is, they can choose to transmit a mix of more than one HD or SD program and include data services over their delivery channel. Contemporary compression equipment can usually facilitate the transmission of one HD program and another SD program of low-resolution, slow-moving content (like weather radar) over a broadcast channel. Emerging advanced compression encoder/decoder technologies will enable delivery of even more programs and services in a broadcast channel.

Digital, expressed in its most fundamental meaning in electrical engineering, is the use of discrete voltage levels as contrasted with continuous variation of an analog voltage to represent a signal. Figure 1.1 shows the same signal in analog and digital form. This simple analog 0.0 to 1.0 Volt "ramp," when converted to digital,

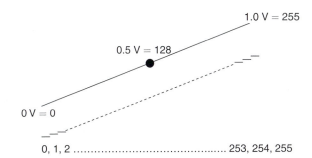

FIGURE 1.1 *Comparison of Analog and Digital "Ramp'" Signals*

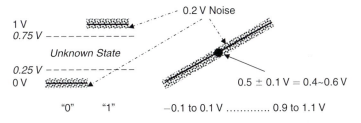

FIGURE 1.2 *Impact of Noise*

can be represented by a series of numbers, i.e. 0, 1, 2... up to a defined number. In this example this is 255. This creates 256 discrete voltage levels. Generally, exponential powers are used, creating 2, 4, 8, 16 distinct voltage levels and so on.

One primary advantage of using digital technology is that digital signals are more resistant to noise than analog signals. As shown in Figure 1.2, for a digital signal as long as the voltage level is above the 0.75 V threshold, the signal will be interpreted as a digital "1". Similarly, if the voltage level is below the 0.25 V threshold, it will be interpreted as a digital "0". Hence, the 0.2 V of noise riding on a digital signal has no effect on the data value. The picture, sound and data will be perfectly reconstructed.

However, in the analog domain, if the actual value of the voltage at the 0.5 V point on a ramp signal that is corrupted by 0.2 V of noise is measured, it will vary between 0.4 and 0.6 V. Hence, this analog signal value is significantly less precise than a digital "1" or "0". In fact the noise will be annoyingly visible on a display.

Another important distinction between analog and digital television, as mentioned earlier, is the composition of a horizontal scan line. As illustrated in Figure 1.3, analog NTSC display lines are presented as a continuous trace on a display. DTV lines consist of discrete, individual pixels. With the migration away from CRTs towards LCD, DLP and plasma display technologies, the concept of lines and pixels is

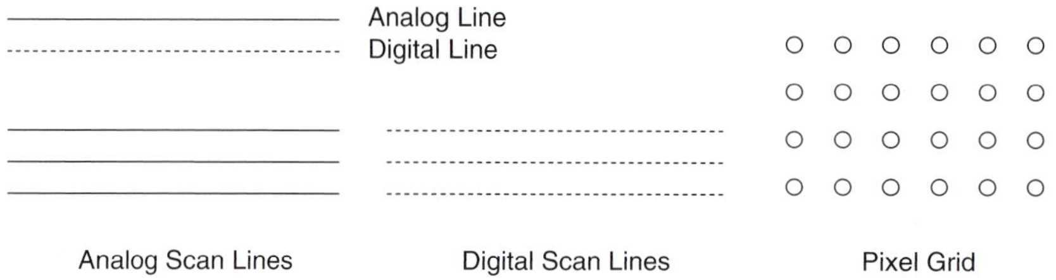

FIGURE 1.3 *Analog and Digital Scan Lines*

implemented as a matrix-like structure, often referred to as a pixel grid. These modern displays now have one native resolution, whereas a CRT could inherently display many different combinations of numbers of lines and pixels.

Standard Definition

SD is only associated with digital television—it does not apply to conventional analog TV. This is an important distinction, though people in the industry loosely exchange the two terms. Standard definition television (SDTV) has the same 4:3 aspect ratio as NTSC. While the exact number of active NTSC lines (480, 483 or 486) can vary, for ATSC SD transmission the picture always contains 480 active lines. For SD resolution with 4:3 aspect ratio, the source content has 720 pixels per line and the transmitted picture frame normally has the center 704 of these pixels. However, all 720 pixels may be sent as well.

> The number of active lines for NSTC and has been described as 480, 483 and 486 lines depending on which "standards" document is referenced. However for SDTV the number is fixed at 480 in the ATSC standard.
>
> The distinction between 720 and 704 horizontal pixels for an SD line is based on the technology used in digital displays or for analog CRT displays respectively.

SD content has been stretched to fill a 16:9 display. This results in a loss of horizontal resolution and the picture looks distorted.

Enhanced definition television (EDTV) is the term used to indicate widescreen, high frame rate, progressive scanning. These standards are extensions of SD and (similar to SD) define 960 and 968 samples per active line for 16:9 aspect ratio pictures.

High Definition

By now, everyone has become familiar with widescreen television displays. In the U.S., they are synonymous with HD content. Yet in Europe, widescreen TV has, until recently, offered no more resolution (just more pixels horizontally) than conventional analog television. As will be discussed in Chapter 2, the development of HDTV was a global technological battlefield, and Europe's lack of support for HDTV in light of historical events was understandable. Until recently, European broadcasters and consumer electronics manufacturers felt that consumers were satisfied with widescreen SD and weren't concerned about image resolution. To influence acceptance of HDTV, the World Cup 2006 broadcasts were an HD showcase in Europe and around the world.

HDTV is digital and defined as double (at a minimum) the resolution of conventional analog TV in both the horizontal and vertical directions. Pixel resolution can be either 1920 × 1080 or 1280 × 720. The geometry of the display is always in a 16:9 widescreen aspect ratio, more like a movie screen and closer to the natural field of vision. Image scanning for each picture is either progressive (line after line) or interlaced (odd lines then even lines). The number of pictures sent per second can vary as well. Audio is CD-quality multi-channel, cinema surround sound.

Chapter 3 will delve deeply into the fundamentals of DTV technology. For now, it is sufficient (but very important) to realize that the HD, SD and analog television formats are three different things.

Going HiDef

The starting gun in the global race to develop HDTV standards is generally attributed to efforts by NHK in the 1970s to gain worldwide acceptance for its Hi-Vision analog HDTV system. In the U.S., it would be fair to say that it began with the creation of the Advanced Television Systems Committee (ATSC) in 1982 and reached "official status" in 1987 when the FCC created the Advisory Committee for Advanced Television Systems (ACATS).

A decade later, "The Advanced Television Systems Committee Digital Television Standard" was formally adopted by the FCC. The motivation to develop HDTV in the U.S. was varied, and depending on viewpoint, was to:

- Replace antiquated NTSC technology
- Quell the threat of losing TV spectrum to mobile services

- Provide a stimulus to U.S. consumer electronics manufacturing

- Prevent a Japanese or European system from setting the U.S. standard

- Keep over-the-air broadcasting competitive and slow the loss of viewers to cable

NHK's efforts to establish an analog HD production standard rather than garner a consensus and create a global HD production standard as intended, ignited a war. Many participants in the European and U.S. television industry, content creators, broadcasters and consumer electronics manufactures became concerned about the Japanese HDTV threat. Chapter 2 will go into more detail about the history of HD standards development and the implementation of DTV.

A classic catch-22 scenario that included production, transmission and consumption issues has contributed to the length of the transition to digital broadcasting. Stakeholders can be grouped into content distributors, content producers and consumer equipment manufacturers. The delay can be attributed to the following factors:

- Broadcasters were not rushing to convert to digital transmission capabilities and installation of an HD production infrastructure in 1998 when the first broadcasts took place. HD production equipment was scarce and when available, expensive. If there was little hope of attracting advertisers without viewers, why invest considerable sums to convert to HD?

- Independent content producers and TV production houses shied away from HD production. HD video tape recorders and cameras, especially lenses, were expensive. And why produce something that will not be widely broadcast and if it is, few will see in all its HD, 5.1 surround sound glory?

- When the first HD broadcasts began in late 1998, few consumers had HDTV receivers. The first sets were projection TVs, large, heavy and expensive, from $3,000 to $10,000. If there was little or no HD programming available, why build receivers that are virtually useless and very few will buy?

And so it progressed, with some forward-looking broadcasters steadily increasing HDTV content, gradually educating others about the experience, with others waiting to see.

A decade has passed since the transition to digital broadcasting began and only in 2006 have the sales of DTV receivers finally exceeded sales of analog TVs. Though that may seem like a slow adoption rate, DTV consumer uptake has actually outpaced the introduction of color television, VCR's and personal computers.

Broadcast Engineering and Information Technology

Modern broadcast operation centers are in many ways huge data processing centers. As a result, along with the media industry transition to HDTV and digital technology, a new engineering discipline is evolving. It is the consummation of the marriage of broadcast engineering and information technology. This new technology discipline, "media systems engineering," encompasses the creation, assembly, distribution and consumption of digital content. It includes traditional broadcast engineering and has added network and storage technology, computer platforms, software applications and security.

> In this book, generally, a reference to information technology or IT will also include all aspects of computer science, networking/storage and security. The individual terms will be used when discussing topics specific to a particular discipline.

The union of these technologies is somewhat like the mixing of oil and water. Broadcast engineering and information technology cultures and business models are fundamentally different.

For example, in the consumer space, televisions are purchased with the intent that they will last seven or more years. They are expected to be reliable, turn on like an appliance, rarely break and never require system upgrades. However, when compared with a personal computer, PC hardware is usually out dated after a year and a half. Operating systems are upgraded regularly. Programs freeze up and sometimes crash. The "blue screen of death" is not a welcome sight.

Differences between Broadcast Engineering and Information Technology
Jargon

Terms used in a broadcast engineering context do not always have exactly the same meaning when used in IT. A "port" in broadcast engineering is an audio, video or control connection. In IT, "port" means a network connection. This distinction is particularly confusing when discussing media servers, since they have both kinds of ports!   CONTINUED ▶

CONTINUED ▷

Support

Broadcasters cannot tolerate any kind of disruption to a program that is on-air. 24/7 vigilant support personnel must be instantly available to correct any problem. IT support often relies on email or the Help Desk and a less-than-instant response time.

Upgrades

Computer systems are upgraded every few months and patches installed almost daily. Once a piece of broadcast equipment is installed and commissioned, because of the around-the-clock nature of broadcasting, opportunities to upgrade equipment are rare and must be scheduled so as not to interfere with operation.

Equipment Lifetime

With the need for 100 percent reliable operation, once broadcast equipment is installed, working properly and doing the job it is required to do, it will continue to be used in some way and rarely be discarded. PC hardware becomes obsolete about every three years. Without replacement, new applications will run with less than acceptable response and performance, if they run at all.

For many years, analog audio and video have been converted to digital signals and distributed around a facility as serial data. For example, audio, video and graphics processing systems convert analog signals to digital, process the signals, distribute them throughout the infrastructure and eventually convert them back to analog for NTSC transmission.

With the compression of audio and video required for digital transmission, the capability of transferring appropriately sized media files over a network can be implemented in broadcast operation centers. File-based media can now be stored economically on servers rather than on video tape. This leads to non-linear workflows, where more than one production process can access a clip simultaneously. Time is saved and more can be done with the same amount of personnel.

As digital media infrastructures grow in size and complexity and integrate diverse technologies, the design, deployment and support of these systems becomes increasingly difficult. Facing the reality that expertise in all technologies integral to media systems engineering cannot be mastered by any one individual, coordination of departmental competencies is critically important.

Media System Technologies

Dividing the role and relationship of various technologies and areas of expertise in a complex infrastructure aids in conceptualizing and understanding the relationship among the various subsystems. In broad terms, digital media systems and broadcast operations centers can be characterized as consisting of four layers: physical, media network, application and security.

At the physical layer, media is in a real-time state. Responsibilities in a digital facility continue to include transmission, network traffic, systems engineering and other traditional engineering departments.

The use of networks and storage throughout a facility in a media network that transfers and stores compressed data is an area of expertise that is growing in importance in a Broadcast Operations Center (BOC).

Software applications run on various computer platforms that control playout, ingest and graphics automation will be installed, configured and tested. The need for security requires a highly skilled and knowledgeable group of IT security experts.

Each of these four layers requires the expertise of experienced professionals. Successful media systems engineering demands that these varied systems and the technologists who design and support them, work together as a cohesive unit.

Communication

As broadcast infrastructures become more complicated and system resources more interdependent, the amount of communication necessary to design, install, commission and support them is becoming virtually infinite. In the analog past, with a single technical department responsible for a system, the communication channel was innate and wide enough to get the job done. Today, with numerous technical department involvement and the large amount of detailed information to be conveyed, sufficient technical communication has become increasingly difficult.

Ad hoc procedures may be developed that circumvent established communication channels in order to get a system operational or to stay on the air. Silos of information and expertise inhibit a full scale system overview and make infrastructure design and support difficult.

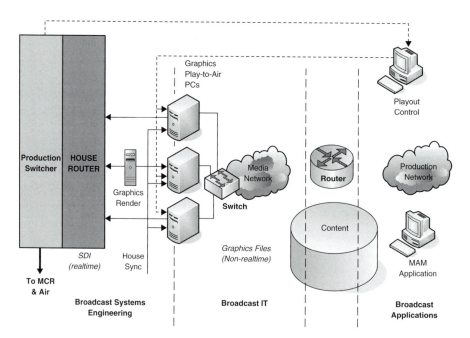

FIGURE 1.4 *A Converged Broadcast and IT Graphics System*

Consider the graphics program control room infrastructure in Figure 1.4. Traditional broadcast system engineers are experts when it comes to production switchers and audio and video routing. Similarly, the broadcast applications experts are a programming group. In between is a new technical domain, Broadcast IT Systems, a place where both IT and broadcast engineering are used.

If there is a malfunction somewhere in this graphics infrastructure, neither the broadcast systems engineering, network engineering or broadcast applications departments individually posses all the required expertise to solve a system problem. It will require competencies from more than one technology department and a coordinated team effort. Support problems can arise if an application programmer tries to debug a network routing problem or if a systems engineer tries to troubleshoot an application problem. Therefore, communication and teamwork are essential.

Team Building

To focus only on the technology—and not on the organizational impact the transition has in a broadcast organization—would be to ignore a potential source of long term problems. This new era, where no one person can master all technologies sufficiently, has intensified the need for coordinated technology teamwork.

A team of people who are probably unfamiliar with working together will be assembled for projects crucial to the facility's digital transition. Teams composed of people who can see the opportunities in the future and who embrace change will transfer much needed enthusiasm to all personnel on the project team.

The best teams are generally built by careful selection of personnel, have worked together in the past and have clearly defined roles and goals. For example, the DTV transmission standard was the culmination of a decade of effort by engineering teams that had been working together at developing HDTV, first as teams within their own organizations, then, in the first round of ATSC testing, as members of competing consortiums, and finally, as one cohesive engineering team, the Grand Alliance.

With so many different experts involved in interdepartmental teams, it can be difficult to coordinate all the available knowledge. There will be a mix of "experts" in each discipline. Experts have a tendency to emphasize what they know and not admit to what that they don't know. But even if an expert knows 90 percent about something, there is still 10 percent of their area of expertise that they are ignorant about.

Experts from different fields may be working on a problem that requires expertise from all of their specialties. If each are 90 percent knowledgeable but are lacking in communication skills, maybe only 75 percent of the knowledge required to successfully attain a goal may be pooled. This can compromise the potential for success.

The challenge is to create a collaborative environment such that these four experts can work together to attain 100 percent of the required knowledge to get the job done.

To help open communication channels, there is a need to include all stakeholders, systems designers, consultants, system integrators, implementation teams, support personnel and users in the design process while systems and workflows are still in the conceptual stage. An organization should strive to migrate from a reactive, fireman, hero culture and evolve to a proactive, team-oriented, long-term vision. This process can be aided by using a technology and organizational strategic roadmap.

A Media Business Technology Strategy Map

"Strategy Maps," by Kaplan and Norton (*Harvard Business School Books*), describes how an organization can develop a strategic capabilities roadmap that evaluates personnel expertise and plans a way to migrate the organization to the desired competencies necessary to navigate a technology disruption. This analytic methodology can be applied to the transition to digital broadcasting.

Figure 1.5 is a strategy map that charts specific actions to take, how they interrelate and how they help an organization attain its business goals. There are two motivating opportunities for increased revenue with the transition to digital broadcasting. Clearly defining an approach will help in attaining this goal.

On the one hand, reducing operational expenses will impact the bottom line. Increases in production efficiency, streamlined workflows and tight integration of infrastructure with operational processes will lead to the ability to create more content in less time. This reduces costs and increases ROI in production infrastructure.

The other side of the business equation is to increase revenue. Income is directly proportional to "consumption" (the act of watching a program), increased market share and higher advertising rates. Unique features and graphics create a noticeably higher quality product and can differentiate one broadcaster's brand from another.

Using the strategy map approach, management can evaluate the organization's technical capabilities and identify areas that need strengthening to support present and future technology based initiatives.

Digital Workflows

As broadcasting evolves to a digital infrastructure and media systems engineering, the changes in technology are so fundamental that there is an opportunity to coordinate the numerous processes, resources and workflows that comprise broadcasting under one enterprise-wide conceptual paradigm. Because the digital transition has exponentially increased the complexity of a broadcast infrastructure, the workflows and methodologies of the analog past will not suffice.

Workflow and technology improvements implemented during the transition to digital, can enable more efficient production processes. This is especially important

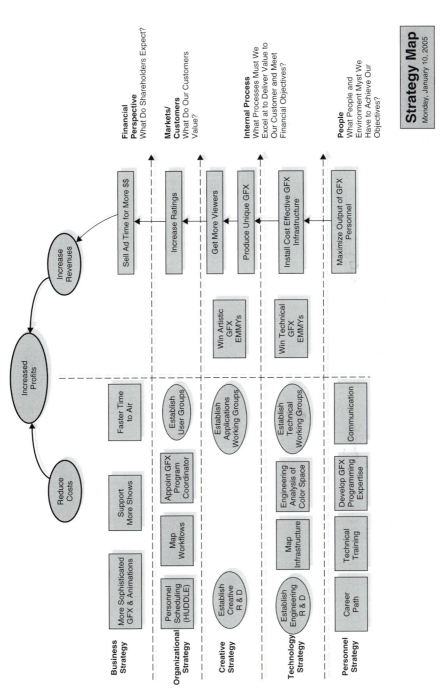

Strategy Map
Monday, January 10, 2005

Financial Perspective
What Do Shareholders Expect?

Markets/Customers
What Do Our Customers Value?

Internal Process
What Processes Must We Excel at to Deliver Value to Our Customer and Meet Financial Objectives?

People
What People and Environment Myst We Have to Achieve Our Objectives?

Increase Revenues

Increased Profits

Reduce Costs

Sell Ad Time for More $$

Increase Ratings

Get More Viewers

Produce Unique GFX

Install Cost Effective GFX Infrastructure

Maximize Output of GFX Personnel

Win Artistic GFX EMMYs

Win Technical GFX EMMYs

Faster Time to Air

Establish User Groups

Establish Applications Working Groups

Establish Technical Working Groups

Communication

More Sophisticated GFX & Animations

Support More Shows

Appoint GFX Program Coordinator

Map Workflows

Personnel Scheduling (HUDDLE)

Establish Creative R & D

Map Infrastructure

Engineering Analysis of Color Space

Develop GFX Programming Expertise

Technical Training

Establish Engineering R & D

Career Path

Business Strategy

Organizational Strategy

Creative Strategy

Technology Strategy

Personnel Strategy

FIGURE 1.5 *Strategy Map*

with the increasing need to repurpose content for multi-platform delivery over the Internet and to cell phones. Production efficiency can maximize the use of production personnel and resources. Besides resulting in an increased ROI, these improvements will help reduce organizational stress during the transition. The transition can be exciting rather than threatening.

Summary

- Digital television is not just better television, but fundamentally different than analog television.

- Many of the problems inherent with analog TV, such as cross color, ghosts and noise, are eliminated with the use of digital technology.

- The term "SD" and "analog" are not interchangeable.

- The transition to digital is occurring in three broad categories: production, distribution and consumption (consumer electronics).

- A natural impact of the transition may be to precipitate organizational evolution.

- Broadcast engineering is still about real-time audio, video and control signal distribution and assembly of program elements but now has added network and storage technology, computer platforms, software applications and security.

- Media systems engineering addresses the integration of traditional broadcast engineering with information technologies.

- Rapidly increasing broadcast system complexity necessitates continual enhancement of expertise by all technical personnel.

- A cultural evolution and migration to a digital mentality is underway.

2 A Compressed History of HDTV

After more than a decade of technological innovation, engineering competition, political maneuvering and finally corporate harmony in the Grand Alliance, the Advanced Television Systems Committee Digital TV standard for terrestrial broadcasts was adopted in December 1996 by the FCC. The members of the Grand Alliance were the last organizations left standing in the competition to develop HDTV. AT&T, Thomson, Philips, MIT, GI, Zenith and Sarnoff had survived the wars and banded together to design, build and demonstrate the prototype HDTV system.

The efforts in these R&D labs were a shining example of team building and organizational cooperation, something not seen since the Apollo project. But the significant difference from the space program was that a major commercial opportunity—the launching of HDTV service—lay before them.

Another decade has passed since FCC adoption of the DTV standard and HDTV is making its way into living rooms around the U.S. (and the world) at an ever-increasing rate. A firm date for analog shutdown, February 17, 2009, has been set in the U.S. More than 50 years of NTSC broadcasting will then come to an end and the transition to digital broadcasting will be complete.

The Road to HDTV

NHK in Japan began working on high definition television in the mid-60s and developed the MUSE (MUltiple Sub-nyquist Encoding) "HiVision" system. MUSE was targeted at satellite distribution of HDTV because the bandwidth required for HDTV was believed to be too great for over-the-air service.

In the early 1980s, HDTV was in the R&D stage. CBS, NHK and major Japanese manufacturers pushed SMPTE to adopt an 1125-line analog HD production standard, and eventually succeeded with the ratification of SMPTE 240M, an analog HDTV production standard. In Europe, development of the EUREKA Project MAC (Multiplexed Analog Component) HDTV system began in 1986.

The U.S. lagged far behind in HDTV development. Consumer electronics (CE) manufacturing had moved mostly offshore, since the American CE industry was dominated by Japanese companies. With the loss of manufacturing, there had been major cutbacks in U.S. CE R&D. In the 80s, it appeared the HDTV would be defined by NHK and the Japanese companies.

Pre-Digital U.S. Systems

By the mid 1980s, there were a few U.S. advanced television R&D projects. SRI's David Sarnoff Research Laboratories, formerly RCA Laboratories—birthplace of the NTSC II color standard—was developing an NTSC-compatible system called Advanced Compatible Television (ACTV). It was a two-phase project, beginning with enhanced definition (EDTV) and, in phase two, HDTV. True high definition television was to have at least twice the horizontal and twice the vertical resolution of NTSC, a 16:9 aspect ratio (as contrasted with NTSC's 4:3) and CD quality stereo audio.

In the spring of 1985, Philips Laboratories launched an NTSC-compatible two-channel HDTV R&D effort. The prototype design used an Intel 8086 microprocessor for side panel stitching and color matching that accomplished the seemingly impossible, invisibly stitching the 4:3 center and two side panels together to form a 16:9 HD image.

NAB sponsored a demonstration of MUSE, over-the air, in Washington, D.C., in January, 1987. The intent was not so much to promote a standard, but to demonstrate the superior quality of HDTV. Congress was so impressed that it energetically urged American companies to develop an HDTV standard.

In 1987, the tide began to turn against the Japanese HDTV system in the U.S. Despite intense lobbying by the Japanese, ANSI declined to accept SMPTE 240M as a national standard. Also in 1987, U.S. broadcasters, in a move to defend the broadcast spectrum from incursion by mobile radio, petitioned the FCC to set advanced television standards. The broadcasters declared they needed to retain their entire spectrum in order to launch advanced television service. In response, the FCC set up an Advisory Committee on Advanced Television Service (ACATS), and appointed former FCC

Chairman Richard Wiley to chair it. The Advisory Committee would prove to be a potent catalyst in stimulating a resurgence of U.S. television engineering.

The use of "advanced television" in the Advisory Committee title, rather than "HDTV," was deliberate. While TV could be improved, or advanced, it was not clear that broadcast TV could reach the standard of high definition. Also, the early thinking focused on an augmentation approach, in which the existing NTSC channel was to be augmented by a second channel, which conveyed supplementary resolution and side panel information. Together, the two channels would provide advanced television. The benefit was that the approach maintained compatibility with NTSC broadcasting. The challenge was that each broadcaster would permanently require twice as much spectrum capacity. More fully occupying the broadcast spectrum fit the broadcasters' political agenda, to defend their spectrum against incursion by mobile telephony.

The Advisory Committee solicited proposals and received 23. Not all were full system proposals, and most existed in concept only. The Advisory Committee decided that, to be seriously considered, a proposal must be built and then tested. In support of the testing, broadcasters and consumer electronics manufacturers, along with the Consumer Electronics Association (CEA) and CableLabs, funded and built the Advanced Television Test Center (ATTC).

At Philips Laboratories, the EUREKA MAC HDTV system was modified to create an NTSC-compatible full HDTV prototype system, High Definition System-North America (HDS-NA). A demonstration consisted of HD encoding, transmission and reception of an NSTC channel with an augmentation channel, and then decoding and reassembling the signals into an HDTV presentation. Subjective tests of image quality were performed and published in the SMPTE Journal in 1991.

Two of the proponents, MIT and Zenith, advocated an alternative to augmentation called simulcasting. In a simulcast approach, the second channel is used to convey an independent advanced television signal which is not NTSC-compatible. To receive advanced television, only the second, simulcast channel needs to be received. The benefit is that, long term, after a transition, only a single channel would be required to support each broadcaster. The concern was whether HDTV could be achieved within a single TV channel.

On March 21, 1990, the FCC ruled in favor of simulcast HDTV, using a 6 MHz channel in the existing VHF/UHF TV broadcast bands. NTSC channels would continue to be broadcast on their current frequency. Broadcasters would be granted a second 6 MHz channel for HDTV broadcasts interspersed among the NTSC channels with no increase in the total spectrum allocated to broadcasting. At some time in the future, NTSC transmission would cease, the total spectrum would be reduced by tighter packing of the digital channels, and the freed spectrum would be auctioned off to the highest bidder for new services.

Proponents were then asked by the Advisory Committee to formally apply for consideration and testing, putting up $300,000 in earnest money to partially defray the cost of testing. What had been 23 proposals suddenly became five serious proposals. Four of the proposals were for HDTV simulcast systems. But then, dramatically just ahead of the deadline in June 1990, a sixth contender, General Instrument (GI), a major cable television equipment supplier, entered the competition with a stunning all-digital proposal.

Gone Digital

It had become apparent to some television engineers that analog transmission would never meet the FCC's interference requirements for advanced television service. This prompted investigation of digital modulation transmission techniques.

GI had a small division in San Diego that provided scrambling systems for satellite transmission of cable television programming. VideoCipher, under the leadership of Drs. Jerrold Heller and Woo Paik, did what was then considered an engineering impossibility. DigiCipher algorithms developed for satellite were adapted to compress a full HDTV baseband signal into a 6 MHz VHF/UHF broadcast channel.

Within a few months of their proposal, GI went private in a leveraged buyout, and Donald Rumsfeld (once and future Secretary of Defense) came in as CEO. Typically companies in an LBO cut back on R&D, but Rumsfeld countered the trend and continued to invest in digital television.

The other HDTV contenders followed suit. Within six months, three of the other four HDTV proposals had switched to all digital, with NHK's Narrow MUSE being the lone analog HDTV holdout. Analog or hybrid systems had been suddenly rendered obsolete, and the U.S. had leapfrogged Japan and Europe into the advanced television R&D technology lead.

In order to hedge their R&D investments and improve their chances of winning the competition, companies formed consortia. GI and MIT formed the American Television Alliance and provided two digital HDTV systems. Zenith and AT&T provided a third, and a team consisting of Sarnoff, Philips, Thomson, and NBC, called the ATRC, or Advanced Television Research Consortium, was the fourth. The remaining two systems were NHK's Narrow MUSE, and ACTV, the enhanced definition system developed by Sarnoff. Testing started in 1991 and lasted through most of 1992.

What were previously just skirmishes now erupted into a full scale battle for the FCC's blessing and HDTV patent rights.

This was the most competitive phase of the HDTV standardization R&D war. Design teams worked around the clock. Each consortium felt they had the best system. Each rooted for problems to beset their competition. Alteration of a scheduled time slot was a political event.

ACTV, with enhanced definition (EDTV) resolution, made its debut and swan song appearance as the first system tested at the ATTC facility. Its purpose was more to be sure the ATTC test bed was fully operational rather than as part of the competition. NHK's analog Narrow MUSE was tested next, and was the first HDTV system tested. The GI/MIT system based on GI's proposal tested third. The Zenith/AT&T system tested fourth, and testing dragged on a few extra weeks to allow correction of an "implementation error." The Philips/Sarnoff/Thomson system tested fifth, and was a few weeks late in getting to the test center, even given the Zenith system delay. Finally, the last system tested was the GI/MIT system based on MIT's proposal.

At the completion of testing, ACTV was withdrawn before a decision was rendered and the NHK analog system was eliminated, as ACATS made the decision that only digital systems would remain under consideration. No clear winner emerged from the digital HDTV systems, as the results were mixed for each of the proponents. The four remaining consortia were asked to submit proposed system improvements and then were to be scheduled for another round of testing.

The Grand Alliance

When it became clear that the Advisory Committee was not going to be able to select from among the digital HDTV systems tested, the four proponents began to negotiate a merger. They realized that a decision would be even more difficult after a second round of testing, since the systems were likely to be even closer in performance after a round of improvements. Proponents were reluctant to undergo additional effort and expense for an uncertain outcome. ACATS Chairman Wiley was informed of the negotiations and wholeheartedly supported a merger. Competitors were urged to form a Grand Alliance and to produce a best-of-the-best system from the four digital prototypes.

After months of negotiation, and some arm twisting by Wiley, the Digital HDTV Grand Alliance was formally established on May 24, 1993. The seven member companies of the Grand Alliance were AT&T, GI, MIT, Philips, Sarnoff, Thomson and Zenith.

The remainder of 1993 was dedicated to defining the Grand Alliance system architecture and then securing approval from ACATS to build a prototype for testing. Two key system elements, audio and transmission, could not be resolved by negotiation within the Grand Alliance, and so it was agreed that a "shootout" in the laboratory would be done for each, with the winner to be included in the Grand Alliance system.

Audio and Transmission Shootouts

The audio shootout occurred first. A multi-channel (5.1) surround sound system was required by the FCC to be included in the Grand Alliance system. There were three candidates: Dolby's AC-3, the MPEG-2 Layer 2 system (also known as MUSICAM) developed by Philips, and MIT's AC system. Subjective listening tests in 1993 at Lucasfilm's Skywalker sound facility indicated that AC-3 was superior in some areas, due to the fact that the MPEG-2 system had a technical flaw and problems with some test sequences. The MIT system was judged to be inferior to both.

With intense lobbying by Philips for a retest, the Grand Alliance had hit an impasse over the audio selection. ACATS nonetheless pressured the Alliance to stay with Dolby, which had apparently won the competition. The impasse was broken when it was agreed that MPEG-2 would be retested following repairs and that it would be a backup for the Dolby system. After retesting, the Grand Alliance issued a statement that the MPEG-2 system was judged to be "equivalent in performance" to the Dolby system.

> In 1997, after the FCC incorporated the ATSC system into its Rules and Regulations, including the requirement for AC-3 audio, MIT filed a lawsuit claiming that the terms of their agreement with Dolby had been breached. After a five-year lawsuit, and just minutes before the jury was to present the verdict, Dolby agreed to pay MIT a $30 million settlement. As part of MIT's policy on technology licensing revenue, MIT's representative to the Grand Alliance—the sole inventor of the technology covered by the MIT-Dolby agreement—was expected to receive more than $8 million.

The transmission competition was between Zenith's 8-level Vestigial SideBand (8-VSB) system and a 32-level Quadrature Amplitude Modulation (32-QAM) system provided by GI. Agreement compliance questions arose about GI, who was forced to use subcontractors to finish their system in time for testing because of a lack of sufficient engineering staff. Zenith, on the other hand, had the resources to carefully tweak its system to perform optimally in the required tests. The shootout occurred in early 1994 at the ATTC, with Zenith's 8-VSB method being declared the winner by a three to one vote.

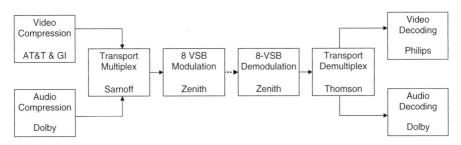

FIGURE 2.1 *Grand Alliance Prototype with Organizational Responsibilities*

The Grand Alliance Prototype

The HDTV prototype system was developed and constructed during 1994. The work was divided among the member companies (see Figure 2.1). AT&T and GI developed the MPEG Video Encoder, while Philips provided the MPEG Video Decoder. Sarnoff built the Transport Encoder, and Thomson the Transport Decoder. Zenith built the modulation/demodulation system. Dolby, who was not a Grand Alliance member, provided the Surround Sound Audio system. MIT's contribution had been its own audio system, which was not selected.

Prototype subsystems were designed and built locally by each member of the Grand Alliance. When debugging was complete, the racks of prototype equipment were shipped for system integration at Sarnoff in Princeton. In order to simplify access by the various teams, the Field Lab, a separate building behind the main laboratory, was used for system integration.

In order to test the 1080 interlaced mode and the 787.5 progressive mode of operation, a real-time format conversion device need to be designed and built. This had never been done before. The Scan Converter would convert 1080i to 787.5p and vice versa in order to drive an appropriate display, usually a Sony HDVS 1080i CRT monitor.

One of the challenges that all Grand Alliance design teams frequently faced was the nonexistence of various pieces of support equipment. HD tape machines, multi-format displays and high speed logic analyzers, to name a few, were expensive and in short supply, if they existed at all. Engineers had to improvise equipment configurations or design and fabricate the circuits needed to verify system performance. A task as trivial today as transferring test files into signal-generating equipment required customized software. In 1994, Windows 3.1 was the latest Microsoft OS.

There were two format converters. The first was developed during the pre-Grand Alliance competitive phase by the ATTC and sourced with Tektronix. It was very expensive, approximately $600,000. Proponents pretty much had to buy it, but were uncomfortable doing so.

The second scan converter whose development cost was shared by GA members lived a storied life. The rack was populated by PCBs designed and fabricated by each member of the GA in their particular area of expertise. Philips did the clock generation, digital to analog conversion and sync boards, GI and AT&T contributed video encoder boards, and Sarnoff managed the group effort. The rack, in various states of completion, made trips to GI in San Diego; Zenith in Chicago; Philips in Briarcliff Manor, New York; AT&T Bell Labs in Murray Hill, New Jersey; and finally to the field lab at Sarnoff in Princeton.

System integration was completed in March 1995, a few months behind schedule, and the prototype was shipped to the ATTC for verification testing. Test results exceeded expectations.

A DTV Standard at Last

ACATS assigned the task of documenting the demonstrated prototype system and drafting a broadcast standard to the Advanced Television Systems Committee (ATSC). In addition to including Grand Alliance HDTV, standard definition formats (SDTV) were added. The success of the GA/ATSC and its imminent adoption by the FCC would give rise to the next phase of HDTV, the beginning of broadcasts and the manufacturing and distributing HDTVs into the consumer market.

In November 1995, ACATS recommended the ATSC Grand Alliance system for FCC acceptance and issued the following statement: "... the Grand Alliance system meets the Committee's performance objectives and is better than any of the four original digital ATV systems; the Grand Alliance system is superior to any known alternative system; and the ATSC Digital Television Standard, based on the Advisory Committee design specifications and Grand Alliance system, fulfills the requirements for the U.S. ATV broadcasting standard."

Done deal? Not so fast. Smoldering behind the scenes, the computer industry contended that, in order to promote interoperability between DTV and PC devices, the ATSC standard should not include interlaced formats and unbelievably, should not include HDTV in the first generation of digital television! They sought to minimize the cost of ATSC-compliant video decoders in PCs, arguing that digital television would be dominated by PC manufacturers, not consumer electronics manufacturers.

Being unsuccessful in influencing the ATSC, the computer industry joined together, formed a consortium and tried a political approach. Reed Hundt, FCC chairman, was sympathetic to the computer industry position in the new era of the National Information Infrastructure and the FCC promoting competition.

The computer consortium lobbied hard through 1996, and the FCC failed to act. FCC Commissioner Susan Ness finally had enough and called for negotiations. In effect, she ordered the warring parties into a room, locked the door and told them they couldn't come out until they had reached a solution. It didn't take long, and at Thanksgiving 1996, the infamous Table 3, which specified the 18 interlace and progressive video formats supported by the ATSC standard, was removed from the draft to-be-adopted FCC regulations. A Christmas Eve present of formal FCC adoption of a broadcast digital television standard ended the arduous HDTV standards quest.

HD and Cable

Although the cable industry actively participated in ACATS, CableLabs conducted cable-specific tests as part of ATTC testing, and GI (now part of Motorola) was a Grand Alliance member, the cable industry was slow to adopt HDTV. Cable was more interested in launching multi-channel SDTV, populating cable systems with 500-channel digital cable. (Perhaps for this reason, the final vote to adopt the Grand Alliance ATSC System was met with an abstention from CableLabs.) The cable industry adopted its own digital standards in 1996.

The Model Station

Launching digital service would be a major undertaking and broadcasters wanted to gain experience with digital television as quickly as possible. Broadcast organizations and the CEA joined together to create an implementation test facility. WRC, an NBC affiliate in Washington, D.C., was selected as the location, and launched HD under the call letters WHD. NBC had been a member of the Sarnoff/Philips/Thomson consortium during the competitive phase but became an adviser with the creation of the Grand Alliance. WHD's mission was to serve as test facility for DTV broadcasting and became known as "the model station." The ATSC prototype that was at the ATTC was now installed at the model station.

Also in 1996, July 23 to be exact, WRAL-HD and WHD-TV went on the air. The landmark event was carefully planned between the Model Station/Grand Alliance and

WRAL/CBS. WRAL in Raleigh, North Carolina, was the first fully FCC-licensed station to go on the air with a DTV signal, and sent HDTV from the start. WRAL-HD broadcast on channel 32 using a Harris transmitter at 100 kilowatts and a 1,750 foot antenna.

Producing HDTV

Now that there was a DTV transmission system, equipment and workflows for a digital HD production infrastructure needed to be developed. Under the Advanced Technology Program (ATP), the National Institute of Science and Technology (NIST) funded a Digital Studio project. Sarnoff was the coordinator, with Grand Alliance members Philips and Thomson augmented by IBM, Sun Microsystems, MCI, Comark Communications and Advanced Modular Systems. NBC and NJN (New Jersey Network) represented the broadcast industry.

The project was an integration of traditional broadcast engineering and information technology. Video was compressed and stored on servers. Search and retrieval software applications were envisioned. MPEG transport stream splicing would permit a network affiliate and downstream stations to pass through network HD programming and insert local commercial spots.

At NAB 1997, the system was demonstrated in a hospitality suite. Seamless MPEG transport stream splicing was a prime feature of the demonstration. Members of the FCC and Congress visited to witness the demo. Senator Conrad Burns remarked that Montana would look great in HDTV.

Not to be out done, Sony demonstrated a baseband studio production suite. Using the recently proposed and adopted 1.5 Gbps SMPTE 292 serial digital interface protocol (which could support uncompressed HD resolution data rates), any thought of implementing compressed domain production disappeared—for many years. A practical means now existed for distributing HD content through a production facility so equipment manufacturers could begin producing SMPTE 292 compliant system resources.

EBU/SMPTE Task Force

Standards bodies did not sit idle after the ATSC DTV system specification was adopted. The Society of Motion Picture and Television Engineers (SMPTE) and the European Broadcast Union (EBU) took take center stage. The formation of the EBU/SMPTE Task Force and their subsequent reports in 1997 and 1998 laid the foundation for the transition to digital Broadcast Operation Centers and production workflows.

The Task Force had two objectives:

- to produce a blueprint for the implementation of the new technologies looking forward a decade or more

- to make a series of fundamental decisions that lead to standards which support the vision embodied in the blue print

So the idea of compressed domain production did not fade away completely. The EBU/SMPTE effort moved well beyond the NIST Digital Studio project, where there was a focus on new business development. Fundamental concepts for production processes were identified and the standardization of technical methodologies begun. Production of compliant equipment was left to manufacturers.

The 85 percent Loophole

A very real fear of legislators in the days after the adoption of the ATSC standard was that constituents who relied solely on over-the-air TV would be forced to buy a new digital TV. And of particular concern were those who would not be able to afford it. In order for a republican democracy to perform as intended, the electorate must be well informed. And TV is an important, if not the primary, means that public becomes aware of the world around them.

Senators Burns of Montana and McCain of Arizona felt that those that could not afford a DTV should not be disenfranchised when NTSC analog transmissions were scheduled to go off the air on New Year's Day, 2007. Each introduced measures to require NTSC transmission to continue until either only 5 or 15 percent of a Designated Market Area (DMA) were unable to receive DTV programming. The final legislation settled on 85 percent DTV penetration. At that time, the unused spectrum was to be surrendered and subsequently auctioned by the FCC.

Funds to be raised by the spectrum action became a hot topic. Why wait to turn off NTSC? Predictions of upwards of $30 billion from the auction could be used to reduce the national debt. Some money could be tithed for use in purchasing DTV equipment by the less fortunate.

Ever at issue was exactly what constituted 85 percent DTV reception capability. Did this mean when DTV purchases constituted 85 percent of the people in a DMA? Or did it mean that when DTV signals reached 85 percent of a DMA? Yet most of America got its TV via cable. So how does cable fit into this equation?

Such indecision continued for nearly 10 years after the Grand Alliance ATSC system was adopted by the FCC. Should cable DTV be considered part of the 85 percent?

Should those that cannot afford it be furnished a DTV receiver? Should analog conversion of DTV be counted towards the 85 percent? And on and on and on ...

HD Goes Coast-to-Coast

HDTV got off the launching pad on October 29, 1998, with John Glenn's return to space aboard the Space Shuttle Mission STS-95. Complete with commercials, interview segments and a two-person news desk, the ATSC HD feed was available to ABC, NBC, CBS and PBS stations coast-to-coast. At the National Air and Space Museum in Washington, D.C., viewers enjoyed the HDTV experience in the IMAX theatre.

ABC aired "101 Dalmatians" in HDTV on November 1, 1998. CBS followed this with a broadcast of the Bills versus the Jets on November 8. Sony equipment dominated the broadcast infrastructures.

What's the Hang Up?

Problems stalling the transition to DTV created a catch-22 dilemma. Without any HDTV broadcasts, CE manufacturers were reluctant to build HDTV receivers. Why would anyone buy one if there was nothing to watch? But why should a broadcaster incur the cost of sending HDTV if no one would be watching? And why produce content if it won't be broadcast or if it broadcast, would be seen by very few?

On the broadcast equipment front, most production equipment was from Sony and other Japanese manufacturers. The 1080 HDVS monitor was huge and the only true HD monitor available. Sony also produced a multisync monitor that would automatically switch from 1080i to 720p, but with reduced video bandwidth, not the full 30MHz. It was not considered adequate for use in a broadcast facility.

> To simplify DTV receiver system design, the 787.5 line progressive format was modified to 750 lines total with 720 active lines. This allows the same pixel clock to be used for both formats.

Early Deployment Hiccups

In the digital world, there is no "snowy" gradual signal degradation. It is an "all or nothing" proposition. In addition to adjusting for propagation errors, digital systems compensate for transmission errors. But when there are too many errors to correct, the correction process collapses and the screen will most likely go black or freeze. This complete loss of a usable signal is called the "cliff effect."

ATSC HDTV is an over-the-air system. In wide open spaces, signals propagate freely, without large echoes or "ghosts," and the signals can easily be received and decoded. The vast majority of TV viewers live in urban or suburban locales where big buildings cause multi-path signal reflections that produce ghosts on a display. In a city like New York, this spells death to receiving a pristine HDTV signal. All the first-generation receivers in 1998 had difficulty decoding the 8-VSB over-the-air signal in the presence of ghosts.

Some, such as Sinclair, saw a solution in the COFDM system that was developed and in use in Europe. Extensive tests were run to show the superiority of COFDM over the 8-VSB ATSC transmission technology. Had it been a mistake to choose 8-VSB? Had the FCC, which tried so hard to avoid the debacle of color TV standard setting in the CBS/NBC reversal, gotten it wrong again? Or was all of this a stalling tactic to keep from having to spend millions of dollars converting to digital production and transmission infrastructures?

The FCC suffered a major embarrassment in setting the NTSC II color television standard in the early 1950s. Initially, the CBS Line Sequential System was adopted. It required a spinning color filter to produce color television images. NBC worked feverishly to perfect and demonstrate its all-electronic color system. In the end, the FCC had to rescind its earlier declaration and adopt the NBC system.

8-VSB decoder chip designers addressed the multi-path issues. New designs were executed in silicon, and new tests were run. In the end, 8-VSB remained the ATSC terrestrial standard and years later an enhanced version was developed and standardized.

As of 1998, no broadcaster had devised a profitable business model based on HDTV. Many had spent millions converting to digital. The running joke was that only Joel Brinkley, as a reporter for the New York Times and author of "Defining Vision," had made any money from HDTV.

Multicast

The ATSC DTV signal enables delivery of 19.39 Mbps of digital data. This is a fixed rate and the spectrum of the RF transmission channel is always completely filled.

However the content of these bits need not be just the data streams to provide one HDTV service.

Because HDTV programming was not available for the entire programming schedule, it was clear that an opportunity existed to monetize these otherwise wasted bits. Early on, the focus was just for dayparts when not transmitting an HD program, as it was easy for the DTV signal to carry more than one SDTV service. In addition, the number of bits per second needed for HDTV is highly variable and subject to technological advancements.

A company called I-Blast formed a distribution network to financially exploit unused spectrum by broadcasters who did not plan to broadcast HD programming. The business model called for charging viewers for the additional SD programming and data services.

Heated Congressional debate ensued as all hell broke loose. Must broadcasters be required to use their second channel for HDTV or should they be permitted to transmit multiple SD programs and data services? After all, the second channel was granted with the implied intent to do HD broadcasts.

The law simply required "digital" broadcasts of a picture (and sound) equal to or better than NTSC, not necessarily HDTV. Congress decided a five percent levee was appropriate for data services. Eventually, I-Blast succumbed to insufficient enabling technology and bad market timing and abandoned its commercial vision.

DTV Conversion

The FCC established a timetable for conversion to DTV broadcasting, based on market size. By May 1999, all network affiliate broadcasters in the top ten markets were required to be broadcasting on their DTV channel. By April 2005, all broadcasters were required to be on the air using their second channel for DTV.

Cable and satellite service providers were under no requirement to deliver HDTV. However, DirecTV began transmission of one HDTV service in October 1998. HBO followed with HD broadcasts in 1999.

Initial OTA broadcasts were done with little more than a single rack of equipment. HD content was backhauled from the field. Broadcast engineering departments implemented systems of modulation, transmission equipment and DTV-capable antennas.

Infrastructure Construction

Terrestrial broadcasters now faced the task of not only building DTV transmission facilities, but forging digital production workflows, processes and infrastructures. In 1998, HD production equipment was scarce and when available, expensive.

PBS at Braddock Place in Alexandria, Virginia, was a next-door neighbor of the ATTC and had been active in HDTV development. An HDTV origination facility was designed and built to support the November 9, 1998, premiere PBS HDTV broadcast of the HD production "Chihuly Over Venice."

NBC stepped to the forefront in May 1999, when "The Tonight Show with Jay Leno" became the first regularly scheduled series to be broadcast in HD. This required an HD studio set, lighting and HD make-up as well as productions switchers, HD signal distribution, logos and Master Control Room functionality.

ABC experimented with the 720p HD format by broadcasting Monday Night Football in 1999 and the Super Bowl XXIV in 2000. Many felt the 720 progressive format was best for sports programming. Fox went with 480p EDTV.

The Tipping Point

Sports broadcasting has a history of driving the adoption of TV technology. Beginning in the post-WWII era, the local tavern was a gathering place for to watch "the fights" because not everyone could afford a TV. The same scenario was seen with color in the 60s and projection TVs in the 1970s. Monday Night Football became an event at the local bar. Sports bars became big business.

HDTV was waiting for its sports moment ... and it came in 2003.

At the Consumer Electronics Association HDTV Summit in March 2003, Gary Shapiro stated that he believed that ESPN's initial HD broadcasts, beginning with Major League Baseball in 2003, will be "the tipping point" in mass market success of HD. ESPN was committed to HD and constructed and commissioned an all-HD 120,000 square foot digital center, the largest in the world at the time. The studio debut broadcast of SportsCenter on June 7, 2004, stands as a landmark in HD history.

This event was a major step in solving the HDTV catch-22 situation. Consumers now had something compelling to watch. What could look better in HD than sports? The ball was rolling, and equipment manufactures and remote location broadcast truck manufacturers decided now was the time to convert to HD. Broadcasters who had been reluctant to go HD or were substituting 480p EDTV realized that true HD would be necessary to compete for eyeballs and ratings.

The FCC also helped accelerate the transition by establishing a timetable for all new receivers to include ATSC 8-VSB DTV decoders. Similar actions required plug-and-play capability with the inclusion of QAM Cable decoders. Additionally, the FCC urged cable providers to begin supplying HD programming in the top markets.

Spectrum Auctions

The FCC, true to its word, in 2001 and 2002 held the first auctions of returned spectrum in the 746 to 806 MHz (Channels 60–69) range. The total take was $540 million. This spectrum is intended to be leased by its "landlords" and has a strict requirement not to interfere with public-safety services.

Return of unused spectrum began when WWAC in Atlantic City, New Jersey, became the first station to petition for the shutdown of its analog broadcasts in 2002. Since then, increasing numbers of stations have filed for permission to shutdown analog broadcasting.

Another 18 MHz, between 698 and 746 MHz (Channels 52–59), was auctioned off in 2002 and 2003 with a total take of $145 million. Estimates of up to $50 billion have been predicted for the leasing of returned spectrum. Discussions criticized the lack of a hard analog shutdown date for depressing the auction bidding. With no definite date for use of purchased spectrum, it was difficult to winners to form a business plan. On February 8, 2006, President Bush signed the "DTV Transition and Public Safety Act of 2005" into law, closed the 85 percent loophole and established that the shutdown of NTSC will happen on February 17, 2009. This will be the long awaited last day of OTA analog television broadcasts.

Summary

- NHK demonstration of HiVision (MUSE) HDTV at SMPTE in San Francisco in 1981 and kicked off interest in HDTV in the U.S. In 1982 the Advanced Television Standards Committee (ATSC) is created.

- Advisory Committee on Advanced TV Systems (ACATS) created by the FCC and Advanced Television Test Center (ATTC) established in 1987.

- General Instrument announces an all-digital system that fits in a standard 6 MHz broadcast channel in 1990. The era of digital HDTV begins.

- Testing of five competing HDTV systems begins in 1991 at ATTC. By 1993 the competing companies form the Grand Alliance.

- The ACATS final report in 1995 recommends adoption of ATSC system. However, the computer industry and movie industry object and delay adoption until December 1996.

- John Glenn's return to space is broadcast in 1080i on October 29, 1998 and is the first coast-to-coast broadcast in HD.

- First spectrum auctions by FCC begin in 2001.

- In 2006 Congress establishes February 17, 2009 as analog NTSC shutdown date.

3 DTV Fundamentals

DTV is deceptively simple on the system level. But drilling down from functional blocks to implementation and even deeper to theoretical foundations, it quickly becomes obvious that the more you know about DTV technology, the more there is to learn.

This chapter begins to explain the basic principles used to engineer DTV. A big picture, conceptual overview is presented using the Motion Picture Experts Group, Advanced Television System Committee ands other standards as a basis. System-level building blocks of generic algorithms and technology used in a DTV system are described.

DTV employs a layered approach to system design. Four sub-systems are linked together to form a DTV broadcasting system: presentation, compression, transport and transmission.

- Presentation: describes image format and sound spatial imaging

- Compression: reduces data quantity and rate to practical levels

- Transport Multiplex: packetizes audio, video and data; includes assembly instructions for the DTV receiver

- Transmission: adds error correction and then modulates symbols for channel distribution

The traditional transmission channels are terrestrial (over-the-air), cable and satellite (direct to home). New distribution channels are the Internet, IPTV and hand-held devices.

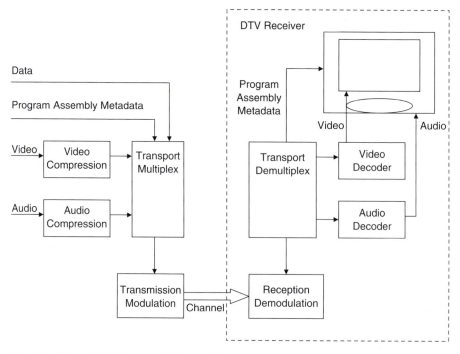

FIGURE 3.1 *DTV Transmission and Reception System*

In the DTV receiver, the broadcast processing sequence is reversed.

- Reception: Signal capture, demodulation and recovery of data packets from the transmission channel;

- Transport Demultiplex: extraction of audio, video and data packets and assembly instructions;

- Decoding: Expansion of compressed audio and video data;

- Presentation: audio and video are synchronized and the complete program is ready for viewing.

Figure 3.1 illustrates a generic end-to-end DTV system.

Engineering Basics

Before even a very high-level description of DTV can begin, a few fundamental engineering concepts must be understood. These are the basic concepts and terminology used by electrical engineers, computer scientists and information technologists in numerous disciplines that are now relevant to the transition to digital broadcasting.

Voltage Levels

A difference in electric charge is measured in volts. Voltage levels are applicable in both analog and digital systems. In analog circuits, signals are dependent on a theoretically continuous range of voltage levels. In practice, this may be 0.000 V, 0.001 V, 0.002 V... The only limit on voltage level discrimination is the sensitivity of a device and the inherent noise level of a technology.

For digital systems, discrete voltage levels represent information. Usually there are two levels, but three, four or more distinct voltage levels are sometimes used by various digital technologies.

Noise in electronic circuits

Every device has an innate amount of electrical noise due to the physical properties of the material used in its manufacture. This noise can become a major problem if it becomes amplified by the circuit.

Noise also comes from external sources such as power lines, cell phones, car ignitions, household appliances, poor wiring or faulty ground connections. Turning on or off electrical devices creates burst noise, while cell phones and computers continuously generate electrical and radio frequency noise.

All of these noise sources are a threat to signal integrity. DTV has engineered solutions to overcome these potential problems.

Units of Data

Digital information is built from simple ones and zeros. Grouping these fundamental building blocks simplifies data processing.

Bits

The term "bits" is a contraction of "binary digits," and derived from converting from commonly used base 10 decimal numbers to the base 2 number system. Binary digital systems represent two "logic" states, a "1" and a "0." A "1" represents an "on" circuit state, while a "0" represents an "off" state when positive logic is employed. The converse implementation is negative logic.

In electronic circuits, these binary states are defined voltage levels. For Transistor Transistor Logic (TTL) technology, a "1" is represented by a voltage level above 2.2 V while a "0" is below 0.5 V. The range between 0.5 V and 2.2 is an indeterminate state and any voltage in this range is said to be in an "invalid" logic state.

Bytes

Eight bits are grouped together to form a byte. Since a bit represents two logic states, a "1" and a "0," eight bits can assume values in a binary number system equivalent to 0 to 255 in decimal. These represent 256 distinct values or voltage levels (2 raised to the 8th power.)

Word Length

Frequently, there is a need to represent more than 256 values, so bytes can be grouped into words. Usually a word is two bytes (16 bits) and can assume 65,536 values in the numerical range from 0 to 65,535. A double word consists of two words (four bytes). These larger groupings simplify programming and numerical calculations.

It should be noted that words are not always a whole number combination of bytes. In digital audio applications, 18- and 20-bit words are frequently used. In digital video, 10- and 12-bit words are common.

Repetitive Signals

The repetitive characteristics of various signals are used in electronic systems. One cycle per second is referred to as a Hertz (Hz), named after the German physicist Heinrich Rudolph Hertz (1857–1894). A thousand cycles is expressed as 1 Kilo Hertz (1 KHz), a million as 1 MHz, a billion as 1 GHz, and so on. Audio signals are measured in Hertz, with normal hearing between the 20 Hz and 20 KHz. Video images have spatial and temporal frequency characteristics as well.

A fundamental use of a repetitive signal in digital circuits is as a "system clock." An example of the use of a system clock specification is by PC manufacturers to describe CPU speed. Today's processor speeds are in the 2.0 to 4.0 or higher GHz range. In digital circuits, a system clock is the timing reference for valid data transfers between components and insures that data is interpreted only as a "high" 1 or a "low" 0, not as an indeterminate value when changing states.

Analog to Digital Conversion and Quantization

Converting from an analog source to a digital representation of audio and video information is the fundamental technology that allows perceptual information to be perfectly transmitted to a DTV receiver. Gathering enough data to accurately record and reproduce sound and images is crucial to the accuracy of this process.

Two factors influence the fidelity of the analog to digital (A-to-D) conversion process. The analog signal has a voltage range that is divided into voltage levels. The number of steps this range is divided into directly influences the accuracy of any digital "sample." The conversion of an analog signal to a digital representation is called quantization. The number of samples over a period of time determines the accuracy of the frequency components of the original signal. This is termed the "sampling period" and is generally related to the system clock.

An illustration will clarify how both of these factors influence the accuracy of conversion of an analog source to a digital representation. Figure 3.2 shows the original signal placed on a grid that divides the signal into voltage levels and sample times. There are four distinct levels in the vertical direction that are represented by two bits. Horizontal divisions represent voltage level samples taken at regular (sample period) clock intervals. As seen in Figure 3.3, the representation of the analog signal in the digital domain is not always very accurate.

Doubling the number of voltage levels (now three bits) and the number of samples per a given interval, as shown in Figure 3.4, improves the accuracy of the conversion. But there are still a few samples that are not very accurate.

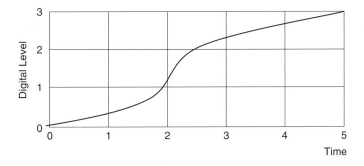

FIGURE 3.2 *Original Signal and Voltage Level/Sample Grid*

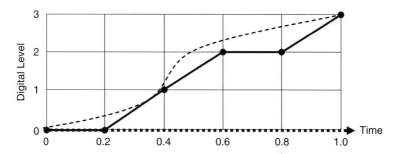

FIGURE 3.3 *Digitized Signal*

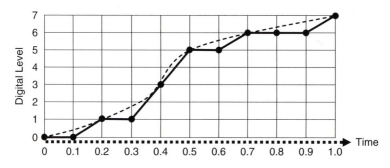

FIGURE 3.4 *Improved Digitization*

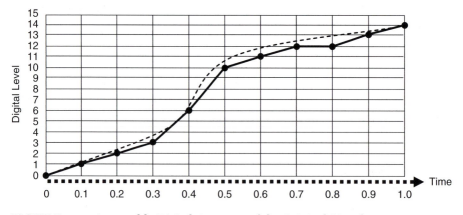

FIGURE 3.5 *Acceptable Digital Accuracy of the Original Signal*

By doubling the number of voltage levels to four bits (16 levels), and maintaining the sample rate in Figure 3.3, Figure 3.5 shows how a very accurate digital representation of the analog signal can be realized.

Accuracy comes with a price. If the sample clock is doubled, the amount of data will be doubled as well. The number of voltage levels also influences the amount of data. Double the number of bits and the amount of data doubles as well. In Figure 3.3, six samples of two bits each result in 12 bits, less than two bytes. In Figure 3.5, there are 11 samples of 4 bits each, totaling 44 bits or 5.5 bytes.

A close examination of sample points reveals that rarely do they coincide exactly with a voltage level. These slight inaccuracies are called quantization errors. When a signal is converted to digital and then back to analog a number of times, these quantization errors accumulate and may lead to noticeable degradation of audio and video.

Data Structure and Processing

Bits and bytes are arranged in a manner where certain groupings represent and convey related information in what is referred to as a data structure or object model. For example, an address book data structure may have entries that include name, address, telephone number and an e-mail address in a defined arrangement.

These structures are processed by machines (i. e., computers). These techniques are the foundations of computer science.

Packets, Headers and Payloads

When digital data is transferred between systems and applications, there must be a method to recognize what information is being communicated. Data is often grouped into packets that consist of the actual content of the transmission (the payload) and additional header information that describes the payload.

Streams

Continuous transmission of data is termed a data stream. This data can be asynchronous, at random times; synchronous, with a defined timing relationship (to a system clock); or isochronous, with a defined amount of data sent over a given time period.

Data Buffer

Data is frequently streamed between applications and devices at differing rates. A data buffer is a storage device, often RAM, that stores incoming data at one rate and transfers data out at different rate. Other uses include converting asynchronous data to a synchronous data stream. Buffers are also used to reorder bits, bytes or other data structures.

Parsing

Examining a data stream for defined values in a data structure and then extracting desired information is called parsing. Headers contain file descriptive information and are parsed to determine what action, if any, should be taken with respect to the payload.

Presentation

Presentation is about immersive consumption. Where content (home theatre, kitchen, on an elevator) is consumed and on what device (DTV, PC or cell phone) directly affect the experience. HDTV was envisioned as a large-screen theatrical viewing experience, yet the detail is so granular that viewing on smaller displays can sometimes convey more of a hypnotic, lifelike experience. Surround sound casts the final incantation and immerses the audience.

The reduction to practice of DTV concepts and a design target of producing an appliance-like receiving device constrained by current technological limits has been challenging for all involved. The goal is mass production of a consumer DTV that is at a price point that is within the reach of the masses.

Visual Perception

The eye is limited in its capability to resolve detail. This ability, visual acuity, is based on viewing distance and the resolving power of about one arc minute in the 20/20 eye. In television displays, this characteristic determines the smallest pixel separation that can be perceived at a given viewing distance.

Vision characteristics were exploited during the development of HDTV display formats. There is a direct relationship between image detail, separation of display "pixels" and viewing distance. For each display resolution (explained later in this chapter), there is a distance at which individual pixels cannot be individually perceived. The distance where pixels become indistinguishable is the optimal viewing distance, depicted in Figure 3.6. For HDTV this is about three times the picture height.

Table 3.1 shows the optimum viewing distance based on the eye's ability to resolve visual pixels separated by one minute of arc for various video formats. For equally sized displays, 1080i with 1920 horizontal pixels can be viewed from a slightly closer position than 720p with 1280 pixels per line. For NTSC, a distance of about seven screen heights will make the individual pixels disappear.

For example, when viewing a baseball game in analog NTSC, the names on a uniform are blurred, and no matter how close a viewer gets to the screen, the letters will not get any clearer. But with HD's higher resolution, the letters are clear and legible at the same viewing distance.

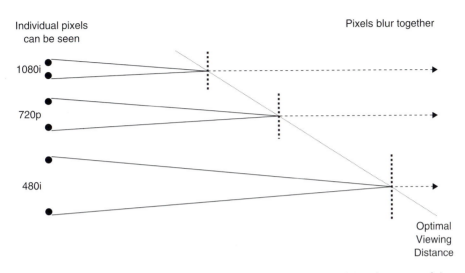

FIGURE 3.6 *Optimal Viewing Distance for Various Screen Sizes (not to scale)*

Diagonal	42″	26″	17″
Height	21″	13″	8.5″
Viewing Dist.	63″	39″	25.5″

TABLE 3.1 *Optimum Viewing Distance Compared to Picture Height for Various Display Sizes*

Visual perception research indicates that the eye has separate cone receptors for red, green and blue. Stimulation by each of these primary colors occurs in a particular proportional relationship for white light.

Luminance Sensitivity

Black-and-white TV represented images as luminance levels. Luminance is the sum of red, green and blue combined with defined weighting factors. Whenever this particular ratio of red, green and blue is present, black, white and gray are perceived.

In analog television systems, the equation for luminance is:

$$Y = 0.30 * Red + 0.59 * Green + 0.11 * Blue$$

Visual acuity varies with respect to luminance. In bright scenes with high contrast, fine details are observable. As the image gets dimmer, contrast lessens and the ability to discern detail is reduced.

	WHITE	YELLOW	CYAN	GREEN	MAGENTA	RED	BLUE	BLACK
Red	*	*			*	*		
Green	*	*	*	*				
Blue	*		*		*		*	

TABLE 3.2 *Additive Color Primary Combinations*

Color Sensitivity

It would be a dull world if black and white were the only "colors" the eye and brain could perceive. Color perception is a combinatorial process of mixing red, green and blue stimuli in proportions other than those that produce white, gray or black.

Visible light is between the wavelengths of 380 nm (nanometer) and 760 nm. The corresponding peaks for each primary color are:

Red	440 nm
Green	540 nm
Blue	700 nm

Additive mixing occurs when light sources are concurrently perceived. When these additive primaries are blended together in varying proportions, different colors are seen.

$$red + green = yellow$$

$$green + blue = cyan$$

$$blue + red = magenta$$

Table 3.2 shows the combinations of red, green and blue that produce the common color bars video test signal. Voltage levels are either 0 V for "off" or 0.7 V for "on" and are mixed to produce fully saturated primary and secondary colors. The absolute characteristics of primary colors (RGB) in image capture and display devices determine the gamut (range) of colors that the display can reproduce.

Video Presentation Formats

A video format consists of an aspect ratio, raster (pixel grid structure), scanning method and refresh rate. The sampling structure of color space for a format can also vary. Analog television had only one video format and one color space sampling structure. There are 18 different DTV formats in the ATSC standard and many more considering satellite and cable!

Aspect Ratio

Motion pictures influenced the display geometry, or aspect ratio, of the earliest TV screens. At the time of the development of black-and-white TV, movies were projected in a 4:3 horizontal to vertical proportion. The TV screen followed suit.

Hollywood progressed over the years to a widescreen aspect ratio (as a response to losing viewers to TV!). The selection of HDTV geometry in the 1980s was again influenced by the film industry. In fact, there was a battle over the proposed widescreen proportions. Many in the film industry wanted a screen proportion greater than 2:1.

Ultimately, a 16:9 aspect ratio was settled upon for the HDTV. This display geometry is considered close to the nominal field of vision. This compromise was influenced by the fact that CRTs with this aspect ratio are more difficult to manufacture than 4:3 but easier than 2:1 or 2.3 :1. And at this time, CRTs were the only available displays. LCD, plasma and DLP were not on the radar screen.

When a 16:9 image is to be presented on a 4:3 screen, a presentation technique must be selected. One option is letter boxing, where the 16:9 image fills the horizontal dimension of the display, and black (or gray) bars fill the top and bottom of the unused display. Conversely, when a 4:3 image is displayed on a 16:9 screen, pillar bars fill the left and right portions of the screen. Framing a scene for aspect ratio interoperability must be taken into account during acquisition and production.

Two examples of display aspect ratio production issues are presented in Figures 3.7 and 3.8, demonstrating that there is a problem in conveying visual information in anything other than the original aspect ratio. In Figure 3.7, the top picture shows a 16:9 scene with two black bars at the outer edges. The middle image shows the area of a 4:3 center that will be "center cut" from the 16:9 image. The bottom illustration shows the resultant image, both black bars are missing!

The "center cut" technique has a high probability of maintaining sufficient visual content to maintain story continuity. But it does not always produce the most relevant visual information.

A technique called "pan and scan", used when converting film to video, extracts the portion of the scene that carries the most relevant information. Each

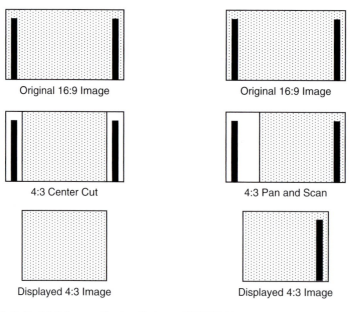

Original 16:9 Image	Original 16:9 Image
4:3 Center Cut	4:3 Pan and Scan
Displayed 4:3 Image	Displayed 4:3 Image

FIGURE 3.7 *16:9 Image Center Cut to 4:3*

FIGURE 3.8 *16:9 Image Pan and Scanned to 4:3*

frame of the widescreen program is examined and the best framing of the content is selected for the 4:3 aspect ratio.

In Figure 3.8, the same original scene in used. In this instance, the right-most 4:3 area is "panned and scanned" from the 16:9 image. The resultant display has only the right most bar.

Converting a movie with an aspect ratio of 2:1 or 2.35:1 for a 16:9 or 4:3 display can lead to similar problems. Visualize a scene where people on the left side of the screen point to an object at the extreme right of the screen. As shown, center cut might actually remove both subjects from the presentation. In this case, reformatting may actually entail cutting the left most portion of the display and then switching to the right most portion, completely destroying the artistic composition and visual impact of the scene.

Another technique that is now rarely used, except for aesthetic effect, is stretching the vertical dimension of a 16:9 image to fill a 4:3 screen. The image is termed "anamorphic." Occasionally an image will be presented in an anamorphic fashion as a result of distribution chain conversion.

Obviously, aspect ratio conversion from a 4:3 image to a 16:9 display also creates problems. How should the extra screen space be filled? If the image is expanded to

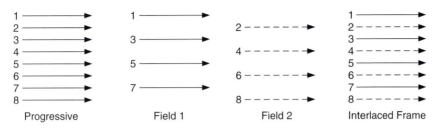

FIGURE 3.9 *Interlaced vs. Progressive Scanning*

fill the display horizontally, information at the top and bottom will be lost. Methods are under development that will solve this aspect ratio display interoperability issue and will be discussed later.

Scanning Methods

The concept of scanning is one of Philo T. Farnsworth's contributions to television technology. An image is scanned from the top left horizontally to create a line. At the end of a line, the scanning beam moves back to the left, but slightly lower than the previous line and creates another line. The resultant display structure is called a raster.

As shown in Figure 3.9, there are two types of scanning, interlaced and progressive. The progressive method scans an image sequentially from line 1 to the final line of the raster to create a video frame. The interlaced method scans odd lines in field 1 and even lines in field 2. Together, field 1 and field two make an interlaced frame. In interlaced scanning, odd and even fields constitute one frame. DTV uses both interlaced and progressive scanning methods.

In television engineering, there is a conversion factor of 0.7—the Kell Factor—frequently used when comparing progressive and interlaced scanning resolution. Therefore, 100 interlaced lines would be about the perceptual equivalent to the human visual system of 70 progressive lines. And because the ratio of 720 progressive to 1080 interlaced is .667, a number very close to the Kell Factor, it can be said that the two HD display formats exhibit nearly equivalent vertical resolution.

Refresh Rate

Television creates the illusion of motion by capturing and presenting still images at a rapid enough rate that the human visual system perceives the successive images as continuous. This rate, the frequency between the display of two still images, is known as the refresh rate and is expressed in Hz or frames per second (fps).

The movie industry uses a refresh rate of 24 frames per second. Any slower presentation of images would produce noticeable flicker and motion judder.

Decades later, 30 Hz (half the AC 60 power line frequency) was set as the frame refresh rate of NTSC I (otherwise known as black-and-white TV). This frequency is above the "flicker" threshold.

Color television, NTSC II (color TV) slightly altered the frame refresh rate to 29.97 Hz. This was done to facilitate maximum audio and video quality while maintaining compatibility with the earlier black-and-white system. This has resulted in DTV frame rates that can be 30 or 29.97, 60 or 59.94. Film frame rates are 24 or 23.98 fps. These numbers are arrived at by multiplying the whole number rate by 1000/1001.

The 1000/1001 rate will no longer be necessary after NTSC broadcasting ends. This idiosyncrasy is typically ignored when counting the number of ATSC display formats, and if considered doubles the actual count from 18 to 36.

Resolution and the Pixel Grid

Resolution levels are determined by comparing the horizontal and vertical numbers in the image pixel grid. NTSC has a 525-line interlaced raster (483 of which have video while in the production process). There are no discrete horizontal elements, and the level of detail is limited only by the bandwidth of the camera and the processing plant, at least until it is converted into digital. Once converted to digital, it is not correct to call the signal NTSC, but standard definition (SD) is appropriate. The digital samples in SD are typically 720 per line. So once converted, the SD line resulting from a NTSC plant can be thought of as comprised of 720 horizontal pixels. However, the 525 lines are broken down into two fields of 262.5 lines (odd and even) in analog, and only 480 are part of the active video. The grid-like structure that this defines is termed a frame. Digital STDV is usually 720 × 480, but lower resolutions can claim this name as well.

> Display formats will always be expressed in pixels per line by lines per frame. So, 640 × 480 is 640 pixels per line with 480 lines per frame. Frame refresh rates specify the number of complete frames. 60p denotes 60 progressive frames per second while 60i denotes 30 frames per second where each frame is comprised of two interlaced fields. One field consists of odd lines the other of even lines.

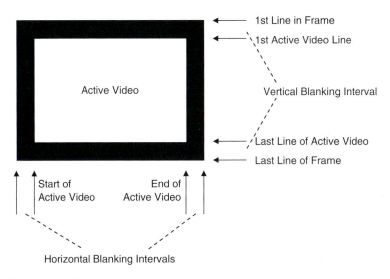

FIGURE 3.10 *Blanking Intervals and Active Video Area*

It is important to understand that the number of pixels and lines in an image format is not really a statement of the image resolution. Image resolution is actually dependent on the entire signal processing chain.

Synchronization

The timing relationship of the scanning process that produces pixels, lines and a display raster (pixel grid) must be unambiguously established. The number of pixels and lines specified by video format designations, 1920 pixels × 1080 lines or 1280 pixels × 720 lines, define the active pixels and lines in a display. But the actual scanning numbers for each video presentation format on a display are 2200 pixels × 1125 lines and 1650 pixels × 750 lines respectively.

The area where pixels and lines are inactive (not used in image capture or display) are called blanking intervals. The inactive pixels in a line make up the horizontal blanking interval and the inactive lines are the vertical blanking interval. Figure 3.10 illustrates the relationship between active video, blanking intervals and a complete frame.

Synchronization pulses establish the timing relationship between lines and a full frame. The vertical sync pulse marks the start of a frame. The horizontal sync pulse marks the beginning of a line. They are generally referred to as H and V signals.

In a production environment, the H and V signals are distributed along with audio and video signals on individual cables. The entire broadcast infrastructure is timed to a "house sync."

Video displays require H and V signals to properly display an image. If either signal's timing is incorrect, the vertical and/or horizontal blanking intervals may appear as black bars on the display. Professional video monitors frequently have dedicated inputs for sync signals.

In analog NTSC, H and V signals are combined into a composite sync and added to the video signal (in particular, the luminance component). This maintains a real-time correlation between video information and image presentation. Then the complete audio and video program is transmitted to the receiver. There, the composite sync is used to maintain display synchronization.

Digital television takes a different approach. A tri-level sync pulse has been developed, with a 0 voltage crossing that facilitates the increased timing precision needed for high definition display alignment. Tri-level sync can also be mixed with the video signal.

It is important to understand that there is a fundamental difference between analog and digital television systems in the way that sync is conveyed to the receiver. While NTSC combines and transmits composite sync with the video, DTV eliminates the H and V blanking intervals during compression. Hence, as will be discussed during the compression section, there is no real-time correlation between video data and image presentation that is inherent in the DTV signal once the image has been compressed.

Pixel Squareness

Computer and network interoperability was addressed during the development of HD and DTV. Refresh frame rates of 72 Hz for PCs versus 60 (59.94) or 30 (29.97) Hz, progressive rather than interlaced scanning and "pixel squareness" issues were resolved with varying degrees of success.

Square pixels are defined (in DTV standards) as when the number of horizontal to vertical pixels is in the same proportion as the display aspect ratio. For example, 640 × 480 is the VGA computer display format, which presents visual information in a 4:3 aspect ratio. 640 divided by 480 is 1.333... or 4:3, the same as the display aspect ratio. Hence, the pixels are said to be square.

For HD formats, both 1920 × 1080 and 1280 × 720 are in the same ratio as the 16:9 display aspect ratio. Therefore, HD formats employ square pixels.

However, there are essentially two frame sizes for digital SD, 720 × 480, and the ATSC 704 × 480. (The other raster in the ATSC standard that is arguably SD is 640 × 480, which was added for computer compatibility, but it is seldom, if ever, used.) Since a 640 × 480 raster creates square pixels, it is obvious that neither of the DTV SD formats do. Further, as these formats can be either 4:3 or 16:9, the pixel shape is not constant.

If video is to be displayed on a computer display, a non-square pixel format must be converted to square or the image will be distorted. This is a complicated conversion and introduces spatial and temporal artifacts. When an image has detailed or rapid motion, refresh rate, raster and color space conversion produce very visible and unacceptable artifacts.

Pixel squareness is extremely important during production when creating graphics on computer systems and then compositing them on video. A simple solution is to create graphics using a "canvas" that is the same display format as the intended display.

Sampling and Colorimetry

Analog NTSC color implementation employed a form of compression based on visual sensitivity by limiting the bandwidth of chrominance signals while using maximum bandwidth for luminance. Exploitation of this fundamental physiological characteristic, that the eye is less sensitive to color detail than it is for luminance (brightness) detail, has been carried over into subsequent DTV systems.

Considering the breakdown of a visual image into a raster, a camera or display device scans the continuous analog image in discrete points of color. In television jargon, it is termed 4:4:4 image sampling when red, green and blue (RGB) values are established for each point in the pixel grid. For a 1920 × 1080 raster of 2,073,600 pixels, there will be a value for R, G and B at every pixel, for a total of 6,220,800 values. At 10 bits per color, at a 30 times per second refresh rate, the data rate is more than a 1.866 Gbps.

This high data rate necessitates data reduction wherever possible. While cameras and displays utilize RGB color space, because of the difference in the eye's sensitivity to color and luminance, RGB is converted into luminance and color difference components for transmission.

Figure 3.11 shows a partial section of lines. In the 1920 × 1080 raster format, each line has 1920 red, green and blue pixel samples. These RGB samples are transformed into Y, luminance and color difference signals U (R-Y) and V (B-Y).

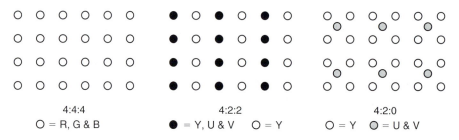

FIGURE 3.11 *YUV Color Space Sampling Methods*

FORMAT	DISPLAY PIXELS	4:4:4 (RGB)	4:2:2 (YUV)	4:2:0 (YUV)
1080i (1920)	2,073,600	6,220,800	4,147,200	3,110,400
720p (1280)	921,600	2,764,800	1,843,200	1,382,400
480i (720)	345,600	1,036,800	691,200	518,400

TABLE 3.3 *Number of Pixels for Different Methods of DTV Video Color Sampling*

This data reduction is applied to video processing in two different ways and is known as a color space sampling structure. One method is used during production with the intent of maintaining the highest video quality with the associated increase in data volume. Another is used in transmission and further reduces the amount of data necessary to produce an image of the highest perceptual quality.

Values for Y are calculated from RGB for every pixel. However, for U and V depending on the sampling structure, values are only calculated for a required pixel. So for 4:2:2 sampling, the RGB data is ignored and discarded for every other pixel on a line. This sampling structure is used in studio and production processes.

If every other line (1, 3, 5, etc.) is RGB color sampled, then both color frequency response and color data is reduced. This method of color sampling is termed 4:2:0 and is used in transmission of DTV.

Table 3.3 compares the size of video data for HD and SD formats.

This reduced color bandwidth is still below the visual detail sensory threshold. In other words, an RGB image transformed to YUV will have imperceptible information removed because the eye is less sensitive to color detail than it is to luminance detail. But these video data volumes and the resulting data rates are well beyond those that can fit into a standard 6 MHz broadcast channel without some kind of compression.

For all the success attained in the quest for visual fidelity, content production is concerned with acceptance of "the look" of a production. For a live event, no doubt a perfect visual rendition is desired. But for some productions, an edgy, artsy look may be more compelling. The film industry has gone so far as to promote a film look as more appealing for dramatic productions for television.

An alternate method of specifying color uses hue, value and saturation (HVS) rather than RGB. Hue is the actual color (wavelength) of the light source. Value is the amount of brightness, the luminance, or in other words how black or white the color is. Saturation is the amount of color present, such as the same hue and value green, but pale or intense.

The HVS system is used in NTSC analog systems. Color information is conveyed via a 3.58 MHz color sub-carrier. The phase of the sub-carrier, with respect to a defined reference, determines the hue (color). The amplitude of the subcarrier corresponds to the saturation. Value (luminance) is represented by the voltage amplitude. The luminance value is added to the color sub-carrier for color TV. In a black-and-white TV receiver, the color sub-carrier was beyond the system frequency response.

A problem with NTSC is that the color sub-carrier reference signal timing can vary from receiver to receiver and the bandwidth for color signals is very limited. This will produce slightly different colors. Hence, NTSC has been dubbed "Never the Same Color."

DTV technology uses both RGB primaries and the HVS methodologies. Digital television produces true color because the chrominance information is deterministic. It does not vary from receiver to receiver.

Matrix mathematics is used to convert RGB to luminance (Y) and the color difference signals, red—luminance R-Y (U) and blue—Y (V). (There are slight differences between U and R-Y and V and B-Y, but they are beyond the scope of this book.) The equation for producing Y (luminance) in HD systems, based on SMPTE240M is:

$$Y = 0.212\,R + 0.701\,G + 0.087\,B$$

The color difference signals (U,V) are produced in a similar fashion. Figure 3.12 shows the RGB and YUV waveforms for the standard color bars test signal produced by matrix color space conversion.

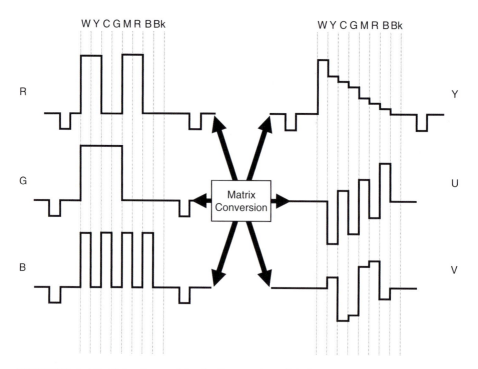

FIGURE 3.12 *Color Space Matrix Conversion of Color Bars (Letters indicate colors: White, Yellow, Cyan, Green, Magenta, Red, Blue, Black)*

The resultant YUV color wave forms are converted back to their original RGB color space for presentation by the display device.

The conversion matrix used in HDTV has been altered to better fit modern camera and display systems. Another correction translates RGB values to better fit the color characteristics of a display technology. These "gamma" values are applied to RGB signals by using look-up tables for each display type. Gamma information is conveyed in the DTV digital data stream.

Maybe 1080i, 720p or even 1080 60p is not detail enough. Theatrical productions are using 2 K and 4 K for digital cinematic presentation. With the emergence of free downloadable content, the only viable business model for the movie industry may be to supply content in a format a viewer cannot get at home via OTA, cable or satellite: a cinematic, immersive experience.   CONTINUED ▶

CONTINUED ▶

A session at IBC in 2005 featured a glimpse into the future. 3-D presentations of clips from *Star Wars* and other movies were stunning. Watching the recently fully restored *Wizard of Oz* was an amazing sensual experience, having only seen it on the tube all my life. Maybe the future of HD is taking us to NHK's *Super Hi-Vision*... 8 K resolution using the new extended X, Y, Z color space with 22 speakers. All other formats will pale in comparison to this experience.

Audio Formats

In television circles, audio has been called many things similar to the illegitimate sibling of video. Witness the miniature speakers in most TVs. Even with the advent of stereo audio, TV speakers have not seen a great deal of improvement. Sound is an integral part of any dramatic presentation. Emotional responses are evoked by musical scores. Sound design and transition effects improve the overall immersive effect of DTV.

When surround sound is used during DTV broadcasts, any discrepancy or deviation from a realistic presentation is even more evident and annoying than with analog TV. The HDTV visual experience is so lifelike that any false location cue or temporal displacement of sound will not feel or sound right. The spell of the immersive experience will be broken.

Engineers are imaginative. Just as DTV video exploits the characteristics and limits of vision, DTV audio systems exploit the auditory system.

Audio Perception

Analogous to the human visual system, the human auditory system has three components; biological, neurological and psychological. The biological component consists of the outer ear and the inner ear. In the inner ear, physical sound vibrations in the air are transformed to electrical nerve impulses, the neurological component. When the nerve impulses reach the brain, the "psychoaural" component interprets the information.

Similar to the eye's visual acuity and color sensitivity capabilities, the ear exhibits limited perceptual characteristics. Frequency response is analogous to the range of light wavelength sensitivity. Volume (loudness) sensitivity is similar to luminance (brightness), while frequency discrimination is similar to visual detail resolution.

Frequency response of the ear is between 20 Hz and 20 KHz, although the upper limit can dip beneath 15 KHz as an individual ages. The dynamic range (volume sensitivity) of the ear is 1,000,000 to 1 (or 120 db).

> Very young children with unimpaired hearing can respond to frequencies in the range of 20 to 20 KHz. Few adults can detect much sound energy above 16 KHz. Nonetheless, 20 KHz is often touted as a speaker design goal. High fidelity presentation of sound will approach a range equivalent to the ear. Sound encoding systems such as Dolby AC-3 sample the audio at rates sufficient to enable capture of sounds higher than the highest perceivable frequency.

Important aspects of aural perception in surround sound implementations are the ability to localize sound and discriminate frequency, as well as the sensitivity to volume. Localization is accomplished by the brain's processing of inter aural delays and differences in sound volume at each ear. Frequency is discriminated by the biological geometry of the cochlea, where small hairs are stimulated by different frequencies. The intensity of the vibration is proportional to volume.

The auditory system can resolve spatial location within one degree of accuracy. Differences in the volume and subtle time delays in the moment that a sound arrives to each ear are processed and facilitate locating the source in the mind's perception of reality.

Figure 3.13 illustrates various volume and frequency characteristics of aural spatial localization ("imaging"). Volume levels are represented by V and propagation time by T. For a sound source that is directly in front of the viewer, the volumes and times are equal for both ears (V,L = V,R and T,L = T,R). The illustration depicts the differences that enable sound localization when volume and propagation time are not equal at each ear.

Audio Presentation Formats

With the advent of DTV, the inclusion of 5.1 multi-channel surround sound capabilities enables a theatrical experience in the home.

Multi-channel DTV audio employs five full range (20 Hz to about 20 KHz, if technically feasible) sound sources and a Low Frequency Effects (LFE) channel, limited to frequencies at or below 120 Hz. These LFEs are called "dot-one." The limited frequency response of the LFE requires less data.

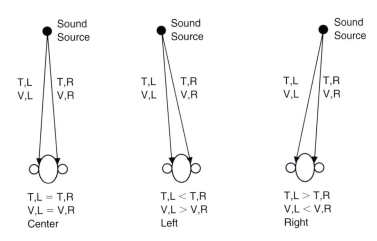

FIGURE 3.13 *Spatial Localization of the Ear*

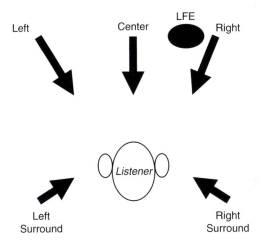

FIGURE 3.14 *Sound Source Locations for 5.1 Surround Sound*

The LFE speaker is meant to convey "feeling" that fits the dramatic action. In this way, an explosion in a movie can be felt. And wouldn't it be amazing to feel the stadium "shake" after a big play! A LFE "sub-woofer" can actually be placed just about anywhere, not necessarily in a front right position.

Various formats of audio presentation are described in a simple manner. 5.1 denotes five full range speakers with a LFE, as shown in Figure 3.14. A 2.0 designation is used for stereo. Figure 3.15 shows how the LFE only passes audio below 120 Hz while the other speakers pass everything above.

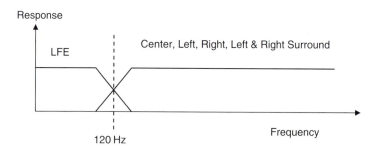

FIGURE 3.15 *Frequency Response Characteristics (after AES)*

A major problem broadcasters now face is how to process and convert different audio configurations, 5.1 or 2.0 (stereo), so they are pleasantly presented on all DTV audio systems. For example, after watching a movie segment and becoming immersed in the aural experience, a cut-away to a commercial not produced in 5.1 will jar the senses. It is worse for news, remote broadcasts, viewer call-in or other ad-hoc, less-than-ideal audio sources. In the past, small speakers masked these quality differences, but surround sound accentuates them.

Compression

Audio and video DTV compression techniques were developed based on studies of human perception. Centuries of studying human perception have taught researchers what is perceived and what isn't perceived. For example, the eyes can only separate detail at a given viewing distance according to well-known mathematical relationships. Similarly, our ears can hear notes only if they differ by a certain frequency. There are many other known characteristics of aural and visual perception that are exploited by compression algorithms.

When confronted with the challenge of getting an HD picture with six channels of audio into a 6 MHz transmission channel, there was only one option: data reduction. A full bandwidth HDTV picture occupies 1.5 Gbps, well beyond the capability of a 6 MHz transmission channel. Data reductions of 50:1 for video and 12:1 for audio are common.

However, there are issues that are particular to compression systems. An encoding and decoding cycle is called a compression generation. In each generation, unperceived information is discarded and cannot be recovered. At some point, multiple compression generations will lead to noticeable artifacts. This has an impact on content production and distribution.

Compression and Presentation Fidelity

The effectiveness of compression algorithms with respect to perception is inversely related to the quality of the presentation device. Information removed during the compression process will be masked by the inadequacies of consumer-quality display and speaker technology. But, with professional grade, full bandwidth speakers and 30 MHz video bandwidth HD displays, information removed during compression will be noticeable. For example, in scenes of high complexity such as rain or crowds, motion artifacts that would be hidden in low quality, smaller displays may become observable in a top-of-the-line, large screen display. Consumer electronics manufactures may not design to the highest technical fidelity but opt-down for lower cost and, amazingly, higher consumer satisfaction. Most people do not have golden eyes and ears and cannot tell the difference between a 23 MHz and 30 MHz display.

Compression engines—circuits and algorithms that process raw audio and video—are divided into two broad categories.

- Lossless compression reduces the volume of data and, when reconstructed, restores it to its original state, perfectly, without the loss of any information

- Lossy compression discards data based on auditory and visual sensory characteristics and limits. Because of the sensory dependency, lossy encoders are called perceptual coders. When reconstructed, the sensory information is virtually indistinguishable from the source

There are many methods of compressing digitized sounds and images. JPEG (Joint Picture Experts Group) concentrated on still images. The Motion Picture Experts Group began development of MPEG-1 in 1988 and froze the standard in 1991. MPEG-2 was standardized in 1994. MPEG-4 video was next and had two versions. The latest from MPEG is documented as MPEG-4, Part 10.

A benefit of modular DTV system design is that the compression method is interchangeable in the overall system. The only requirement is that the appropriate compression decoder resides in the processing device.

DV (Digital Video), IMX, HDV and XDCAM are among the other compression formats used in video systems. Of particular interest is the recent adoption of two

	SIMPLE	MAIN	4:2:2 PROFILE	SNR	SPATIAL	HIGH
Low		4:2:0 352 × 288 4 Mbps		4:2:0 352 × 288 4 Mbps		
Main	4:2:0 720 × 576 15 Mbps	4:2:0 720 × 576 15 Mbps	4:2:2 720 × 608 50 Mbps	4:2:0 720 × 576 15 Mbps		4:2:0, 4:2:2 720 × 576 20 Mbps
High – 1440		4:2:0 1440 × 1152 60 Mbps			4:2:0 140 × 1152 60 Mbps	4:2:0, 4:2:2 1440 × 1152 80 Mbps
High		4:2:0 1920 × 1152 80 Mbps	4:2:2 1920 × 1080 300 Mbps			4:2:0, 4:2:2 1920 × 1152 100 Mbps

TABLE 3.4 *MPEG Profiles and Levels*

The basic conceptual functional blocks of an MPEG video encoder are illustrated in Figure 3.16.

Group of Pictures

A group of pictures (GOP) is a sequence of compressed video frames of a defined pattern and length. The pattern and length of a GOP impact the amount of compression and video quality that is attained during the compression process.

Frames are compressed as either:

- I frames: Intraframe, a frame that is encoded independent of any other frames

- P frames: Predictive, encoding is dependent on a previous I frame

- B frames: Bidirectional, encoding is dependent on previous or subsequent I or P frames

A GOP defines a repeating sequence of I, P and B frames. I frames are larger than P frames and P frames are larger than B frames. Therefore, the number of P and/or B frames in a GOP influences compression gain. More B frames enables higher compression ratios.

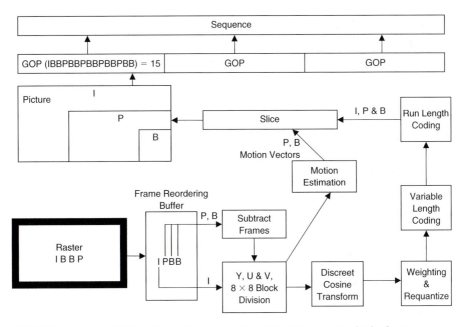

FIGURE 3.16 *MPEG-2 Video Encoding Simplified Conceptual Block Diagram*

A "Long GOP" of 15 frames (I B B P B B P B B P B B P B B) is commonly used. This equates to a half second for 1080i at 30 Hz or one quarter of a second for 720p at 60 Hz. One half second has been defined as the maximum acceptable time for channel switching. This is important because switching from one MPEG source to another, such as for commercial insertion or when changing channels, will cause disruption of the data flow and noticeably affect the video.

Because they are completely self contained, this disruption can be minimized by switching at an I frame. Hence, they are often referred to as anchor frames. I-frame-only compression is used to maintain image quality and to attain frame accurate editing.

Compression Steps

A determination is made based on GOP structure as to how the current frame will be encoded. If it is to be a P or B frame, the raster is subtracted from the anchor (I) frame or, for a B frame, from either an I or P frame.

Compression of a video frame to produce an I frame is the simplest to describe because it is compressed without reference to any other frames. (P and B frame compression will be described later.)

The raster is then divided into blocks of 8 × 8 pixels. Y, U and V are processed separately.

The next steps reduce the amount of data. These are:

- Discrete Cosine Transform

- Weighting and Requantization

- Variable Length Coding (Entropy/Huffman coding)

- Run Length Coding

Discrete Cosine Transform

The Discrete Cosine Transform (DCT) converts 8 × 8 blocks of pixels into 8 × 8 blocks of frequency coefficients. Interestingly, the 8-bit pixels result in 11-bit coefficients! But the coefficients will ultimately facilitate a higher compression ratio because many of the coefficients will be zero.

Using an inverse DCT at the receiver, combining the 64 coefficients will result in the original 8 × 8 pixels. This is virtually lossless. But if higher compression ratios are desired or if a constant bit rate must be maintained, coefficient word length will be reduced from 11 bits. This results in data losses.

Weighting and Requantization

Sensitivity to image noise is greatest at low frequencies. This visual characteristic is used to reduce the amount of high frequency information. In other words, since the eye does not see high frequency noise, reducing the high frequency coefficients to zero (or near zero) enables greater data reduction in the next compression step.

As was shown earlier in this chapter, the number of bits used in sampling determines the accuracy of digitized data with respect to the original source. Requantization changes the number of bit-levels (see pages 39–41) and introduces errors. Since these errors are largest in high frequency data, detail will be diminished. The challenge is to keep this quality degradation below a perceptible level.

Entropy Coding

Entropy is a measure of randomness. Entropy (Huffman) coding is employed to reduce data. The method is a form of Variable Length Coding (VLC).

VLC uses the statistical probability of a particular data value to send a smaller amount of data to represent that value. Morse Code uses a similar technique. The letters "E" and "T" occur most frequently and are transmitted as a dot or dash. Less frequently used letters and numbers are a combination of up to five dots and dashes.

Consider the 25-letter sequence:

A A B A C A A A A D A C A A A A C A A B A A A A A

The frequency of each letter is:

A = 19
B = 2
C = 3
D = 1

If each letter is coded using an 8-bit representation, the total number of bits required will be 200 (8 bits times 25 letters).

Using the VLC methodology, a coding tree can be built based on bit decisions by applying the rule that valid code words always end in "0." A tree structure for the above scenario can be constructed as follows:

A = 0	1 bit	1 * 19 = 19 bits
C = 10	2 bits	2 * 3 = 6 bits
B = 110	3 bits	3 * 2 = 4 bits
D = 1110	4 bits	4 * 1 = 4 bits
		Total = 34 bits

The 200 bits required has been reduced to 34 bits and conveys the same information. This is a coding gain of 200/34 or 5.88 (a compression ratio or 5.88:1).

In the MPEG compression process, coefficients produced by the DCT are assigned code words. Use of VLC coding produces a considerable coding gain when applied to the 11-bit DCT coefficients.

Run Length Coding

Run Length Coding (RLC) completes the compression process. RLC takes advantage of the fact that macroblocks will have strings of zeros. Consider a series of data such as:

A   B   C   D   E   F   G   H ...

Because there is no repetition of any character, the only way to convey this information is to send each character, a total of eight bytes.

Now consider the sequence A A A A A B B B, which can be conveyed by A 05 B 03. The number after the character indicates how many times the character is

Frame Number

To be compressed as:

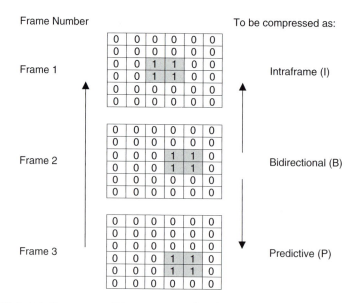

Frame 1 — Intraframe (I)

Frame 2 — Bidirectional (B)

Frame 3 — Predictive (P)

FIGURE 3.17 *Sequence of Uncompressed Video Frames*

repeated. This reduces the amount of data from 8 to 4 bytes and exactly represents the original character sequence.

Exploiting Temporal Redundancy

Redundant information from frame to frame can be exploited to further reduce coded data. Common sections (DCT blocks) of successive frames need only be coded once and then repeated. This is the idea behind P and B frames.

Creation of a P frame begins with subtracting the current frame from an I frame. B frames reference more than one frame, whether I, P or other B frames. Then only the visual information that is different between frames is compressed and transmitted.

In the simplest example, consider the "display" of boxes. As can be seen in the three boxes at the top of the illustration (Figure 3.17), a background of "0" is common in all scenes. A black box (of "1"), moves across the scene. The sequence of frames is I, B, P. After the I frame is compressed, only the differences between each frame need be coded. All the information from a previous scene is constant.

This is done by first subtracting the third scene from the first and then encoding it as a P frame. Figure 3.18 illustrates the process. Only the difference between the frames is compressed.

0	0	0	0	0	0
0	0	0	0	0	0
0	0	1	1	0	0
0	0	1	1	0	0
0	0	0	0	0	0
0	0	0	0	0	0

minus

0	0	0	0	0	0
0	0	0	0	0	0
0	0	0	0	0	0
0	0	0	1	1	0
0	0	0	1	1	0
0	0	0	0	0	0

=

		0	0		
		0		1	
			1	1	

I Frame (Frame 1)   Frame 3   P Frame

FIGURE 3.18 *P Frame encoding*

			1		

FIGURE 3.19 *B Frame Residual Data*

A B frame is produced by coding the differences between the frame to be encoded—in this example, the previous I frame and the subsequent P frame. Figure 3.19 shows the remainder, or "residuals" that are left to be compressed. In this way, B frames are encoded using a minimal amount (less than a P frame) of bits.

Further reduction of data is accomplished by tracking the movement of blocks of pixels. Continuing the box example, the box would only be coded once, along with the direction of its movement. These "motion vectors" describe in x, y coordinates where the box has moved. However, errors are produced by this process. Motion vectors compensate for these errors and minimize the amount of data lost and only the remaining differences (errors) are coded.

As an example, a blue sky is broken down into blocks of pixels. Rather than completely recoding this portion of the image in a subsequent P or B frame, the unchanged block of 8 × 8 pixels can be repeated to reconstruct the sky.

Audio Compression

Perceptual coding facilitates audio compression of data to a manageable rate while still delivering CD-quality sound. Broadcast environments use 48 KHz rather than the 44.1 KHz CD sampling rate. 20-bit samples, frequently used for audio distribution, result in very nearly a 1 Mbps data rate; six channels would require 6 Mbps. Yet AC-3 ATSC compression achieves CD quality sound at 384 Kbps for 5.1 channels!

Aural Perception and Compression Algorithms

The first step in the audio compression algorithm is to divide the frequency spectrum into overlapping sub-bands that follow the physiology of the cochlea. Auditory sensory limitations are exploited when compressing sound. An audio coder will try to compress all sounds, both heard and unheard. Using a psychoacoustic model, sounds that will not be perceived are not coded and hence save bits for more complicated sounds that are actually heard.

Masking

Masking is when one sound hides perception of a second sound. These unheard sounds need not be encoded. Intensity masking occurs when a louder sound renders a quieter sound inaudible. The ear has a varying sensitivity to volume dependent on frequency. Sound that has a volume above the threshold is audible; sounds below the threshold are unheard.

Volume masking (or simultaneous masking) effects occur if two sounds of widely differing volume happen simultaneously or very close together in time. The louder sound will mask a weaker tone as is illustrated in Figure 3.20; the loudest tone (tallest line) in the middle overrides the softer tones (the dotted lines) on either side.

Soft tones that precede or follow the loud tone in time, will also be masked. This is called forward and backward temporal masking.

Frequency masking occurs when two sounds are so close in frequency that the ear cannot hear them separately. An intermediate tone will be produced. This

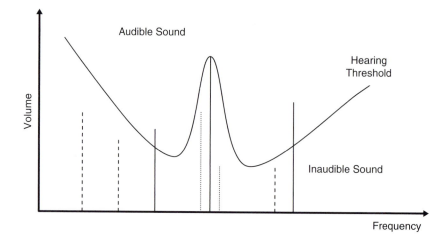

FIGURE 3.20 *Volume Masking*

characteristic is based on the physiology of the ear. In the cochlea, hairs of shortening length are stimulated by sound. When two hairs close to each other are stimulated, the auditory system blends both stimuli into a single sound. Exploiting this characteristics permit a further data reduction by encoding only the sound that the psycho acoustic model predicts will be produced when two sounds of very nearly the same frequency are present. This is represented in Figure 3.21; the sound represented by the dotted line is actually a blend of the two dashed lines on either side.

The psycho acoustic model used is critical to audio fidelity. The model employed is one of the differences between audio compression algorithms such as AC-3 (Dolby Digital) part of the ATSC DTV standard, MPEG 3 (MPEG 1, layer 3) and Windows Media Audio.

Framing

Audio is divided into frames of a constant duration. At a given sampling rate, this produces a constant amount of raw data. The raw audio data is transformed into windows of frequency components. Due to overlapping, similarities between frequencies in neighboring windows, redundant information can be eliminated.

High frequency information is requantized based on the psychoacoustic model. This results in further reduction of the data amount and associated bit rate.

AC-3 (Audio Coder 3) is the audio compression methodology used in the ATSC DTV system standard. AC-3 compression produces audio blocks, five of which are incorporated in an audio frame as shown in Figure 3.22. Frames also contain synchronization and error checking information. Other metadata in the audio stream identifies the number of audio channels and additional audio attributes.

Redundant information is contained in audio blocks. In this instance, only the first block of the frame has complete audio data. Subsequent blocks in the frame use this common information. In this manner, data is further reduced.

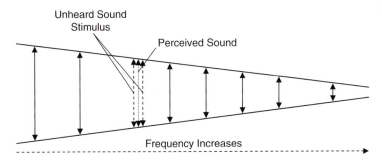

FIGURE 3.21 *Frequency Masking*

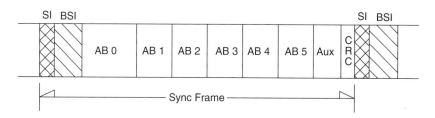

FIGURE 3.22 *AC-3 Synchronization Frame* (From A/52B, Courtesy ATSC)

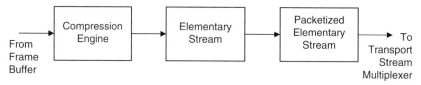

FIGURE 3.23 *Compression Layer Overview*

Compressed Data Streams

The result of the compression process is a continuous flow of audio and video data known as an Elementary Stream (ES). Elementary streams do not have a direct correlation with real time. Horizontal and vertical synchronization signals that are important in presentation do not exist once audio and video are compressed. Because sending each ES separately would result in loss of the audio/video timing relationship, most real-time compression equipment re-associates the elements into a transport stream which carries the Packetized Elementary Streams (PES) as shown in Figure 3.23.

PES packet headers include:

- Packet Start Code Prefix

- Stream ID

- PES packet length

This is followed by the audio, video or data payload bytes.

Additional data fields are placed in MPEG data structures by signaling that an adaption field is present. For audio and video presentation synchronization, presentation time stamps (PTS) are among the additional data fields that can be included in a PES packet header.

Synchronization is maintained by including PTS data in PES packet headers. The system timing relationship is established by the System Time Clock (STC). The STC is a 33-bit word, representing "ticks" of a 90 KHz signal derived from the 27 MHz (encoder) system clock.

Compression is classified as variable bit rate (VBR), which produces constant quality, or constant bit rate (CBR), which produces variable quality.

It is important to understand that variable and constant do not directly refer to the actual compression of a frame. The actual amount of data produced when compressing a frame is dependent on picture content and varies. VBR and CBR refer to the rate that data is stored in the video, audio or data buffer.

Packetized Transport

The next step is to further divide each PES into smaller packets for transport.

There are two types of MPEG streams: Program and Transport. Program streams are designed for use in environments that will rarely corrupt data. Program streams contain a single audio and video program while transport streams may contain numerous programs.

A DVD player uses program streams. As a self-contained device, audio and video data never travels beyond the DVD player, so the potential for data loss is very low.

Transport streams are intended to enable robust delivery of data over channels in noisy, error prone environments. Packets are much smaller than those in a Program Stream and include information that can be used to determine if the packet has been corrupted during transmission.

Transport streams consist of 188 bytes. Figure 3.24 illustrates the packet structure. The first four bytes contain the header information; the remaining 184 bytes are the payload. The first header byte is the sync byte with a value of 47 hex. Location of the sync byte in a transport stream bit stream identifies the beginning of the packet. Header data can be extended by the inclusion of an Adaptation Field and Optional Fields.

A Packet ID (PID) is located in 13 bits of the packet header. Packets from each individual audio or video stream (PES) are assigned a unique PID. This is the number used to keep track of the bits associated with each audio, video and data component of a program.

Multiplex Concepts

To understand how these packets are assembled into a transport stream, the concept of multiplexing—mixing together two or more discrete digital signals into one—will be introduced. Referring to Figure 3.25, consider two digital signals, called A and B. Both

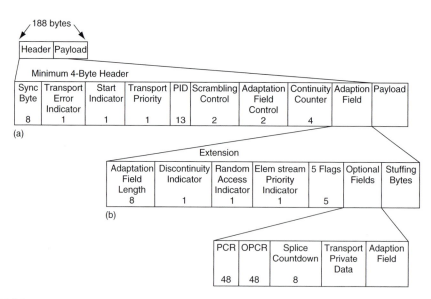

(a)

(b)

FIGURE 3.24 *Transport Stream Packet Structure*

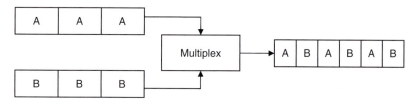

FIGURE 3.25 *Multiplexing Two Data Streams*

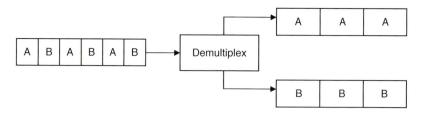

FIGURE 3.26 *Demultiplexing Into Two Data Streams*

of these data streams enter into a multiplexer at the same rate, via dedicated input ports. The streams exit through one port in A, B, A, B order at twice the input data rate.

Demultiplexing is the converse operation. As shown in Figure 3.26, a data stream of A, B, A, B, A, B enters a demultiplexer at a given rate through one port. Two output

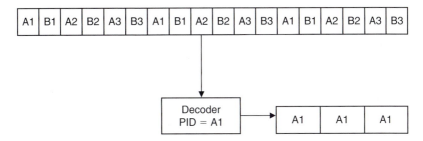

FIGURE 3.27 *Decoding Packets for A1*

signals, A and B, exit the demultiplexer at half the input data rate on dedicated output ports.

In another implementation example, as shown in Figure 3.27, consider a data stream consisting of randomly ordered packets designated A1, A2... B1, B2... where there are multiple instances of each packet. Feeding this stream into a demultiplexer type device, packets with a particular PID can be filtered and assembled into a stream. In this illustration, a decoder filters packets with a PID of A1, and produces a stream of only A1 packets.

Applying this concept to the case of audio and video transport stream packets (Figure 3.28), consider three individual streams of audio and video carried in one transport stream, with an association such that one video PID and one audio PID constitute a program. Three of these program streams (A1, V1), (A2, V2) and (A3, V3) are multiplexed into a transport stream. A transport stream decoder filters audio packets with a PID of A1 and video packets with a PID of V1, producing a program stream with only A1 and V1 packets.

This is the basic premise of program assembly in a DTV receiver. Specific details of how a program is assembled from audio and video packets in an ATSC MPEG transport multiplex will be covered in Chapter 5. But before delving into this complex methodology, it is helpful to examine the original MPEG paradigm used initially by the ATSC.

PSI and Program Assembly

Program Specific Information (PSI) is the MPEG-2 paradigm that facilitates locating the associated audio and video packets in the transport stream. Combinations of audio and video are termed "services" rather than programs. The PSI defines the relationship of a set of tables that carry program assembly information in the transport stream and facilitates construction and presentation of a program.

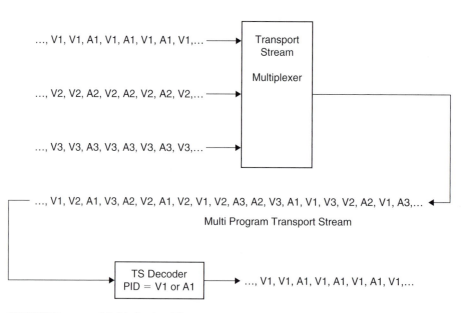

FIGURE 3.28 *Multiplexing Three Program Streams*

The PSI tables are:

- PAT: Program Allocation Table, PID = 0

- PMT: Program Map Table

- CAT: Conditional Access Table, PID = 1

- NIT: Network Information Table

- TSDT: Transport Stream Description Table, PID = 2 (optional)

The PAT, CAT and TSDT have defined, unambiguous PID values. Each transport stream has only one PAT, with a PID of 0. Data included in the PAT are the PID numbers of PMTs. A PMT contains the PIDs of audio and video (and any other program element) that comprise a program service. The PMT contains information that is technically valid until the next PMT table section is received, typically about 0.4 seconds. Accordingly, this is viewed as the "right now" signaling.

When the program is scrambled, the CAT—whose PID is always 1—contains information to enable descrambling and end user authorization.

The TSDT is an optional tool for sending a special set of descriptors that apply to the entire TS multiplex.

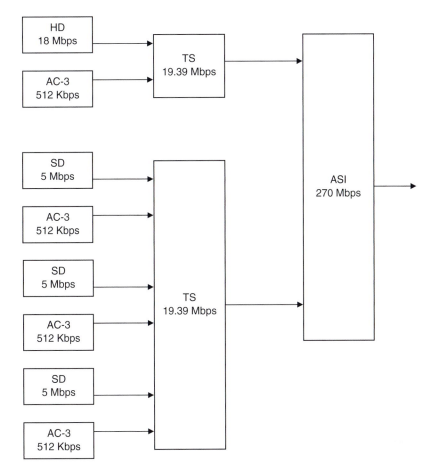

FIGURE 3.29 *Multicast TS Example*

Transport Stream Multiplex

Transport streams are sent at a piecewise constant data rate. Packets of data making up a program can be inserted into the stream up to this rate. For example, as shown in Figure 3.29, if a transport stream has a data rate of 19.39 Mbps, it can accommodate HD video at 18 Mbps and audio at 512 Kbps that comprise one program.

The Asynchronous Serial Interface (ASI) is a method of combining multiple MPEG-2 transport streams into a 270 Mbps serial data stream that can be carried and routed over existing facility serial digital routing systems.

However, Figure 3.29 also shows that three complete SD programs of video peaking at 5 Mbps and audio at 512 Kbps (a total data rate of 16.536 Mbps) can fit in a 19.39 Mbps transport stream. It is this methodology that allows one TV channel to deliver either one HD program or "multi-cast" more than one SD program.

Statistical Multiplexing and Rate Shaping

Since compression bit rates vary based on complexity, much of the time the capacity of a transport stream will not be fully utilized. Figure 3.30 is typical of VBR program data rates in a transport stream. The maximum data rate cannot be exceeded. Properly encoding program 4 will cause the data rate to be larger than this limit. In this case, the bit rate of program 4 will be reduced and audio and video quality will suffer.

Because compression systems can make use of a feedback loop to allocate bits based on video frame content complexity, the peak data rates for each stream can be varied. For example, if coding of SD programs is restricted to no more than 4 Mbps, as shown in Figure 3.31, four complete programs with a total maximum data rate of 19 Mbps (including audio), rather than three, can fit in a 19.39 transport stream.

Figure 3.32 illustrates a statistical multiplex system. Audio and video decoder bit allocation is controlled by the transport stream multiplexer. When a complex scene (lots of detail and motion) needs more bits, the control loop allows that encoder to use more bits when the total bit rate budget is not being exceeded.

This facilitates use of less channel capacity for the same number of programs. For example, 24 programs at 5.5 Mbps occupy eight transport streams and transmission

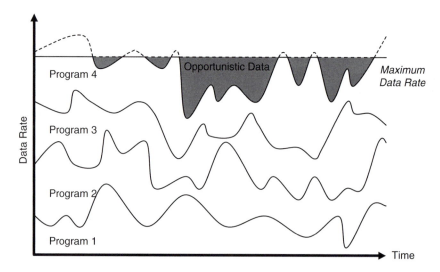

FIGURE 3.30 *Four-Program Multiplex that Exceeds TS Capacity*

channels, whereas at a 4.5 Mbps rate per program, only six transport streams are necessary.

By leveraging the statistical probability that more than 4.5 Mbps will very rarely be required for video compression, most of the time audio and video will be at

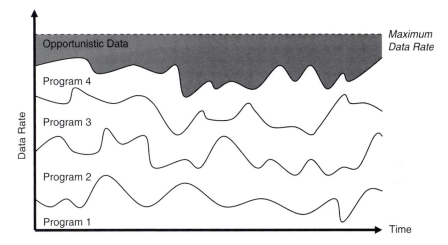

FIGURE 3.31 *Four Program Statistical Multiplex*

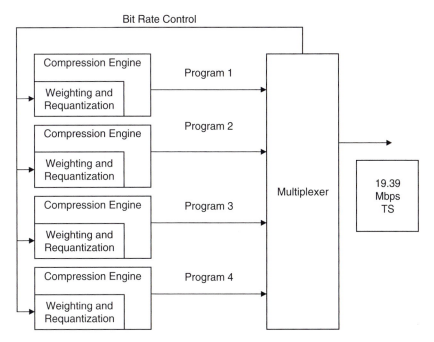

FIGURE 3.32 *Conceptual TS Bit Rate Control System-Level Block Diagram*

optimum quality. However, if all feeds have complicated audio and video, there will not be enough bits available for encoding. Quality will have to be sacrificed to fit the programs into the transport stream.

A way around this is to use a technique known as rate shaping. By transcoding video to a lower bit rate, it can be guaranteed that multiple programs will always fit in a transport stream.

> The fact that cable and satellite service providers are cutting back on the bit rate of terrestrial network and local HD programs may turn out to be an advantage for over-the-air broadcasting. OTA is the only delivery channel that delivers full HDTV quality all the time.

Transmission

For all the talk about "digital" TV, it is somewhat ironic that transmission methodologies are still analog technologies, with a special twist. With exception of quantum physics, it's an analog world.

Transmission is a two step process. The first is data protection (organizing and adding bits), and the second is modulation (creating the symbols).

Data Protection

Data is first conditioned to withstand noise and other impairments. This is important because transmission channels will corrupt data. Since packets cannot be resent (as they can over the Internet), methods must be employed to guarantee valid data is delivered to a DTV receiver.

Data protection includes four key steps (see Figure 3.33):

- data randomizing: spreads data over the full transmission channel

- Reed-Solomon encoding: adds extra information for error correction

- data interleaving: spreads data over time so impulse noise errors can be corrected

- trellis encoding: deterministically maps symbols to voltage levels

Randomization

In technical terms, randomization uses a bit pseudo random number generator, feedback loop and XORs incoming data to scramble the stream. Its purpose is to avoid

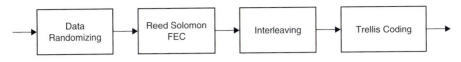

FIGURE 3.33 *The Four Steps of Data Protection*

repetitive patterns and to spread energy equally across the spectrum. The resultant signal is noise-like when observed on a spectrum analyzer.

For example, a bit sequence such as 00 01 00 00 10 00 00, considered two bits at a time, would have five "00"s, one "10" and one "01". This would create a "spectrum" that used one spot five times and the others each once. This is wasteful because much of the full transmission channel bandwidth would be idle most of the time. Also, if noise was in the same spectral location, the data would be badly corrupted.

Now consider the sequence 00 01 11 10 00 11 01 10. All of the possible two bit patterns are used the same number of times. This will maximize use of the transmission channel and minimizes the impact of impulse noise interference.

Reed-Solomon Encoding

Retransmission of corrupted data packets is impossible, so a Forward Error Correction (FEC) technique is used. Extra parity bits are sent with the transport stream packets that allow recovery of corrupted bits. The algorithm is capable of correcting multiple invalid bytes caused by noise burst errors.

A parity bit is an extra bit added to a sequence of bits to have it contain either an even or odd number of "1"s. For example, the bit sequence "0 0 0 1" has one "1". To attain even parity, the parity bit is "1"; or if odd parity is used, the parity bit is "0". This increases the probability that a bad bit in a word will be detected.

However, once a word is identified as incorrect, which bit is bad can not be determined in this manner. It takes a bit matrix and the calculation of parity words to identify the bad bit. Consider the 4 × 4 bit matrix on the left in Figure 3.34.

In the matrix to the right, the bold numbers in the right column and the bottom row are the values necessary to achieve even parity. This produces two parity code words. In this instance "0001" for horizontal 4 bit words and "0010" for vertical words.

Now consider that one bit is corrupted and changes from a 1 to a 0, as in Figure 3.35.

Now the "0001" code word (the right column) for the horizontal sequences has an incorrect second bit and the "0010" code word (bottom row) for the vertical

Bit Matrix

Bit Matrix
with Parity Words

FIGURE 3.34 *Uncorrupted Bit Matrix*

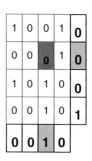

FIGURE 3.35 *Corrupted Bit Matrix with Identifying Parity Words*

sequences has an incorrect third bit. By finding this intersection on the bit matrix, it is determined that the value should be flipped from the incorrect "0" to a "1." Now all the parity check words are correct.

This is a rudimentary description of the FEC mechanism. The implementation in DTV is significantly more complex and capable of correcting multiple bit errors.

Data Interleaving

A complex convolutional byte interleaver disperses data. In other words, whole bytes are divided and time-dispersed sequenced to occur over a defined period. By spreading the data words over time, the number of bits in a word that are corrupted by impulse noise can be limited and remain within the limits of reconstruction techniques. If too many bits in a word are lost, the word cannot be reconstructed. Simply put, data interleaving breaks up words over time. This limits the damage done to any one word.

As can be seen in Figure 3.36, a numerical sequence represented by a "count", when hit by a noise burst will be damaged. Let's say that using RS FEC methods, only one bit can be corrected in a "triple" packet. If the time duration of the noise is only one count, then that error can be corrected. But if the duration is longer, and more than one count is corrupted, data will be lost. So in this example, a noise burst destroys four consecutive positions such that two triples each have errors in two data positions. This cannot be corrected.

1 2 3,   4 5 6,   7 8 9,   10 11 12,   13 14 15,   16 17 18

NOISE
BURST

1 2 3,   4 5 6,   7 ~~X X,   X X~~ 12,   13 14 15,   16 17 18

FIGURE 3.36 *Burst noise corrupts four data words. Two errors per packet, only one error per packet can be corrected*

1 4 7,   2 5 8,   3 6 9,   10 13 16,   11 14 17,   12 15 18 Interleaved sequence

NOISE
BURST

1 4 7,   2 5 8,   3 ~~X X,   X X~~ 16,   11 14 17,   12 15 18 Corrupted interleaved sequence

1 2 3,   4 5 X,   7 8 X,   X 11 12,   X 14 15,   16 17 18 De-interleaved sequence, 1 error, correctable

1 2 3,   4 5 6,   7 8 9,   10 11 12,   13 14 15,   16 17 18 Error Corrected

FIGURE 3.37 *How data interleaving enables correction of noise bursts*

Now consider "interleaving" the count number as shown in Figure 3.37. When this sequence has multiple bits corrupted, it is less likely, when the sequence is returned to its correct order, that more than one count in a triple is corrupted. In this case, the same noise burst destroys four positions again. However, on de-interleaving the intelligible positions into triples, four triples each have one error. One error is correctable, hence the data has been recovered.

Trellis Encoding

Trellis encoding divides 8-bit bytes into groups of 2 bits which produce 3 bit "symbols." These symbols represent eight distinct voltage levels that are used to modulate the RF carrier wave.

The actual numerical and algorithmic implementation to construct these symbols is complex and is tailored to each modulation standard and is beyond the scope of this book.

Digital Modulation

Modulation is the act of varying the amplitude, frequency and/or phase of a radio frequency (RF) wave. The RF wave is termed the carrier because the information to be communicated is coded into the wave itself. Each of the traditional broadcast channels uses a different form of digital modulation (see Figure 3.38):

- Analog modulation: a continuous signal is added to the carrier wave.

- Digital modulation: discrete analog voltage levels representing symbols are modulated on to the carrier wave.

- Vestigial SideBand (VSB): VSB filters out most of the lower modulation sideband. As previously described, data is grouped three bits at a time into a symbol. These three bits define eight voltage levels (trellis coding). Each symbol modulates a carrier frequency. ATSC terrestrial transmission uses 8-VSB.

- Quadrature Amplitude Modulation: Two carrier waves, 90 degrees apart in phase, are digitally modulated. If two bits are used to modulate each carrier, then 16 distinct points are created. This is known as a constellation. The number in front of the QAM is the constellation size. Many cable systems originally deployed 64 QAM and are now shifting to 256 QAM.

- Quarternary Phase Shift Keying (QPSK): A carrier of four different phases is multiplexed to create four distinct data signals corresponding to two bits of information. Direct broadcast satellite systems use QPSK.

Digital modulation techniques are mappings of digital data to analog voltage levels and RF carrier wave phase relationships. Each combination is called a symbol. These voltage levels then modulate a carrier signal, the fundamental technology that has facilitated broadcasting since its inception. Vestigial SideBand (VSB), Quadrature Modulation (QAM) and Quaternary Phase Shift Key (QPSK) used for over the air, cable and satellite delivery channels respectively all modulate analog voltages that represent digital values onto a Radio Frequency carrier wave. Each system has a predefined set of voltage and phase values that represent the "true" value of each symbol. This knowledge is the special twist, as it can be used to decide which symbol was received. Each symbol represents a number of bits.

A benefit of digital modulation is noise immunity. Additionally, some enable compensation for propagation distortions. As described in Chapter 1, analog signals reflect the amount of noise in the presentation of the information they convey. A 0.2 volt amount of noise is noticeable on a 1.0 volt peak signal. On the other hand, the same noise on a two-level 0.0 and 1.0 volt digital signal will not interfere with the complete recovery of the data.

Similarly, analog signals carried on RF waves are subject to noise impairments. If the carrier wave is distorted, it will impact the analog signal. When the signal is demodulated, noise will be present and the presentation degraded. However,

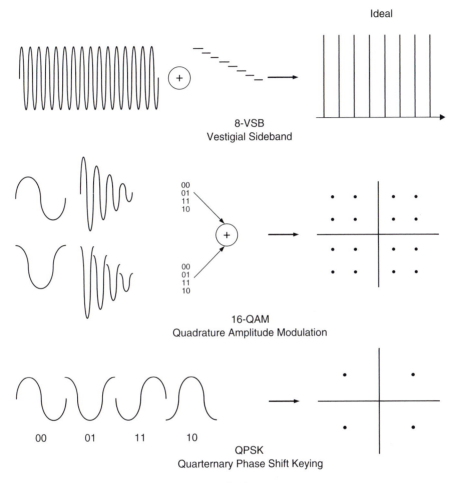

FIGURE 3.38 *Digital Modulation Methods*

modulation of digital symbols is more robust than analog signals and will survive intact with equal amounts of carrier interference.

Mapping the digital values on an X/Y coordinate plane produces a constellation. Figure 3.39 shows the results for 8-VSB, 16-QAM and QPSK.

Figure 3.39 also illustrates the impact on noise on each method of modulation. The illustration depicts an oscilloscope display. On the left side of the illustration are the pristine signals, the right shows the impact of noise on each form of modulation. These signals are still recoverable. It can easily be seen, that as the amount of noise increases, there will be a level where the elements of each constellation are mixed together. At this point, the digital cliff, the data is lost beyond recovery.

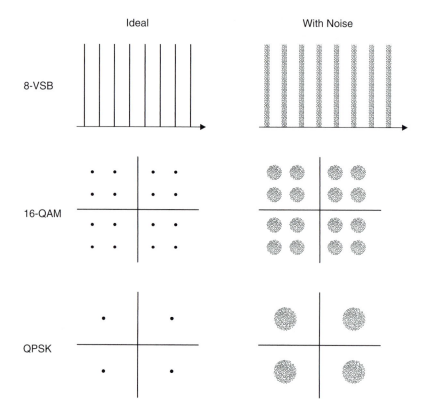

FIGURE 3.39 *Noise expands but does not destroy or impede digital signals*

Summary

- Four sub-systems form a DTV broadcasting system: presentation, compression, transport and transmission.

- Exploitation of the characteristics and limitations of sensory perception are used in DTV presentation and compression systems.

- Packetized audio and video along with assembly instructions are sent to a DTV receiver.

- Digital transmission uses sophisticated method of error protection and correction.

4 The DTV Receiver

This is a very confusing time for DTV receiver purchasers. Although logos identify the compatibility of DTV receivers with different audio, video and data capabilities, few consumers really understand what these features do.

Audio and video compression and forward error correction processing for transmission of a digital television program is a compute intensive, complicated fusion of numerous engineering disciplines, computer algorithms and various technologies. By placing this complicated process on the origination side of the end-to-end DTV system, consumer receivers can be built that are affordable and reliable.

But even with this asymmetric complexity, the Grand Alliance prototype HDTV "receiver" occupied the equivalent space of two refrigerator-sized racks of circuit boards and power supplies. It is truly amazing that in 10 years' time, the entire "guts" of an HDTV receiver has shrunk so much that it can fit inside a 1.5″ by 3″ device that connects to a PC USB port.

There is a fundamental difference between analog and digital television transmission, and a reciprocal, fundamental difference in analog and digital TV receivers. Analog TV transmits both audio and video as one composite signal with an inherent timing relationship. DTV sends packets that must be parsed from a transport stream, decompressed and assembled into audio and video for presentation by the receiver.

A DTV receiver can be thought of as a Digital Signal Processor (DSP) that is finely tuned for audio and video. Consequently, the complexity of the origination systems

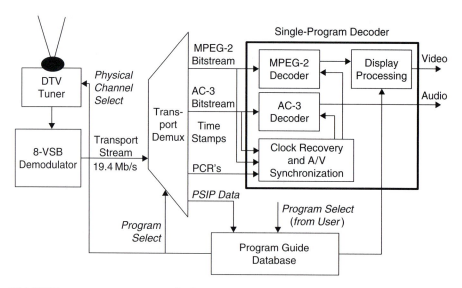

FIGURE 4.1 *DTV Receiver Block Diagram* (From A/69, Courtesy ATSC)

and the simplicity of the receiver are relative. Everything about DTV technology is complicated.

The DTV reception and presentation process is, generally speaking, the reverse of the transmission process (see Figure 4.1):

1. Reception and demodulation

2. Transport stream demultiplexing

3. Decoding and decompression

4. Audio and video presentation

Reception and Demodulation

Digital modulation and data protection techniques enable perfect transmission of audio and video. As described in the previous section, noise immunity of the digital modulation transmission method communicates ones and zeros perfectly, as compared to a noisy analog signal.

In the event that burst or other noise corrupts digital information, data protection techniques, such as FEC processing, fix transmission channel impairments to the data. The signal has to get very bad to be beyond repair.

The number of bits that are corrupted over a period of time is referred to as the bit error rate or BER. BERs are expressed in numbers such as 10 to a negative exponent, such as 10^{-6}. This means that one bit out of 1 million bits will be bad. A transport stream has a data rate of 19.39 Mbps and the 10^{-6} BER would have, on average, 19 bad bits per second.

DTV receivers over 13" are required by the FCC to have ATSC-compliant demodulators. Many manufacturers are also Digital Cable Ready (DCR) although there is no FCC mandate to do so.

Transport Stream Demultiplexing

The demodulation process produces a transport stream consisting of packets of audio, video and sometimes data. Assembly instructions are also present.

DTV is fundamentally different from analog television, audio and video are transmitted without a fixed sequential temporal relationship. The DTV receiver must demultiplex audio, video and data packets and find and interpret the assembly instructions.

Program assembly information in the transport stream, either Program and System Information Protocol (PSIP, discussed in the next chapter) or Program Specific Information (PSI) tables, must be found and interpreted. This information enables parsing the transport stream multiplex and facilitates recovery of audio and video associated with a program. In this way, audio and video packets, each with their own distinct Packet ID (PID), are demultiplexed and sent to the compression decoder.

The recovery steps are:

1. Examine the PAT (the Program Allocation Table always has a PID of 0)

2. Determine the PID of the PMT (Program Map Table)

3. Find the PMT

4. Extract the audio and video PIDs

5. Demultiplex the audio and video (and sometimes data) packets

System timing information must also be recovered. The System Time Clock (STC) in the receiver must be synchronized with the STC that is related to the program audio and video. The time of day is also sent.

Recovered audio and video packets are now sent on to the decompression engines for decoding.

Decoding and Decompression

Decompression is a compute-intense process that takes varying amounts of time. Audio and video packets are processed separately and reconstructed to full-bandwidth, real-time signals. There is a considerable difference in processing times for audio and video.

Audio packets are received in time-sequential order. They can be decoded and presented as a continuous stream. However, video packets arrive in decode order, not the presentation order. This is done to minimize the number of frames that must be stored to perform decompression. In this way, DTV receiver complexity and cost is minimized.

The video frames must be decoded and reordered into their proper time sequential order after the video decompression process is completed. If the receive order of frames is:

I P B B P B B P B B
1 4 2 3 7 5 6 10 8 9

When properly reordered after decompression:

I B B P B B P B B P
1 2 3 4 5 6 7 8 9 10

The baseband video is now ready for real-time presentation.

Program Assembly and Presentation

With analog television, the real-time relationship of presentation of audio and video was maintained in the transmitted signal. In DTV systems, the assembly instructions and system timing are parsed from the transport stream data.

The receiver must present the audio, video and data program elements in the way that the program originator intends. Presentation Time Stamps (PTS), recovered from the transport stream, are used by the receiver to present video and present audio at the correct time.

Receiver Issues

DTV technologies are not 100 percent perfect. There are new problems that broadcasters and consumer electronics manufacturers must address and solve.

Analog TV's reliability and ease of use has accustomed viewers to think of television receivers as an appliance—every time it is turned it on it works and a single push of a button controls operation. DTV broadcasting is still striving to reach this goal.

Reception and Error Correction

Digital modulation has solved many of the analog TV reception quality issues, but problems with burst noise and signal degradation still exist, just as they do with analog TV. The difference is that with digital technology many, but not all, of these transmission errors have been eliminated or can be corrected.

The Cliff Effect

Digital reception is mostly an all or nothing proposition. When too many bits are lost and correction methods fail, presentation generally totally fails. Some reception interruptions can occur when a signal is above but near the threshold. This all or nothing characteristic of digital systems is known as the "cliff effect." As shown in Figure 4.2, this characteristic of DTV systems differs significantly from analog NTSC TV where the picture and sound degrade gradually, ghosts and snow appears while the sound gets scratchy.

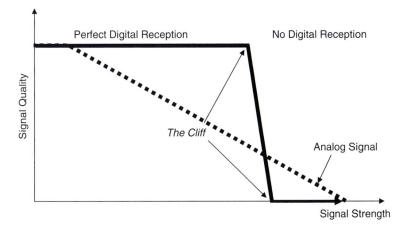

FIGURE 4.2 *The Cliff Effect*

Multipath Reception

Seeing ghosts (a visual echo) on an analog television picture is the result of reflected radio waves creating interference patterns and causing the signal to arrive at the receiver at slightly different times. The effect can be visualized in the following example. Throw a rock into the middle of a lake, and the waves move outward in concentric circles. If the waves bounce off an object, like a boat, they are reflected and crisscross the original concentric circles. Any point in the water now receives both the original and the reflected wave.

Multipath signals in OTA reception exhibit a similar phenomenon. RF signals propagate freely in open space. But in an urban area, buildings reflect the RF signal and reach the DTV at varying times from different directions. This makes it difficult to decode the original digital signal. Adaptive equalizer technology can adjust the parts of the signal arriving at different times to compensate for these reflected waves.

When these impairments are beyond the ability of the signal equalization and error correction algorithms to repair, the DTV receiver abruptly goes black. If errors can be partially corrected, "blocking" or "freezing" of parts of the display may occur. Audio may have clicks, echoes or phasing effects.

First generation DTV 8-VSB demodulators were criticized for their failure to perform in multipath conditions. This gave rise to the COFDM challenge described in Chapter 2. Improved designs in successive generations of 8-VSB demodulator chips (the sixth generation should be available by the time this book is published) has resulted in receiver performance that meets or exceeds the FCC expectations for digital coverage with the allocated transmission power levels.

Audio/Video Synchronization

While audio frames maintain their sequential time relationship, video frames are not sent in sequential order. This leads to very different processing times for audio and video decompression.

Problems can arise with maintaining audio/video synchronization that can lead to severe lip sync problems because of these unequal delays. Although each PES packet for audio and video is marked with a PTS, not all DTV receivers will process this information in the same way.

To make matters worse, there is no guarantee that the audio and video were properly aligned when they were time-stamped by the program originator. Audio and video take different distribution routes in a production infrastructure and even if audio and video are in sync when they leave master control, downstream compression and multiplex processes may introduce timing errors.

In the case of video, the frames are received in their decode order. At the receiver after decompression, the sequence must be returned to its correct presentation order. In this case, there will be up to a three frame delay. This temporal difference must be corrected with respect to audio that is received in sequential time order.

Presentation Concerns

Analog NTSC has one display format. DTV offers more than one. Audio that is transmitted as 5.1 may need to be down-mixed to stereo. This has created challenges in program presentation.

Display Native Resolution

CRT technology can support multi-format scanning. As long as the line and frame refresh rates are within the design limits of the receiver, switching between 1080i, 720p and 480i is possible.

LCD, DLP and other display technologies have a matrix-like, pixel grid physical display structure. There are a fixed number of pixels and lines. The structure is called the native resolution of the display.

Consider the scenario of a display that has 1920×1080 native resolution. If the program image pixel grid is the same as the display native resolution, there is a one-to-one pixel and line correspondence. However, if the program is in a 1280×720 format, a conversion in both the vertical and horizontal directions must be done. This always results in a loss of detail.

This pixel grid conversion problem will always exist because of the fact that different broadcasters will use varying video formats. DVD's add to the problem by introducing 480p and with HD, 1080 24p and 60p formats. The situation is simply a fact of life with pixel grid type displays and underscores the need for high quality (expensive) format conversion and the importance of sitting at the proper viewing distance.

Scanning and Frame Rate Conversion

Conversion from interlaced to progressive scanning and vice versa is not straight forward. As shown in the following conversion scenarios, the accuracy of recreation of

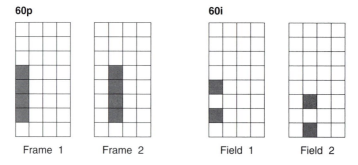

FIGURE 4.3 *Frame Rate Conversion from 60p to 60i*

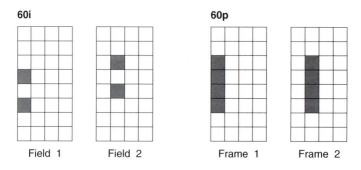

FIGURE 4.4 *Frame Rate Conversion from 60i to 60p*

the image is decreased. Some type of motion compensation must be employed or judder artifacts may appear.

Figure 4.3 is an illustration of a conversion from 60p to 60i (with the assumption of and identical pixel grid display). A vertical bar moves from left to right 1 pixel for each frame, every 1/60 sec or 0.0167 seconds. Converting to 60i, each field occurs at the same 1/60 sec, each frame 1/30 sec.

If pixels are mapped onto successive 60i fields in time correspondences with the 60p source, the top and bottom edge of the bar will be jagged as it moves across the screen.

In Figure 4.4 is a 60i to 60p conversion performed for a bar that moves upward and to the right one pixel in each direction at a 1/60 sec rate. If field 1 and field 2 are combined to form two 60p frames, the motion of the bar will not be distorted and both spatial and temporal resolution will be lost. The edges will be jagged.

Frame rate conversion from film rates or 1080 24P uses a 3:2 pulldown technique. Figure 4.5 shows how a rate of 24 frames per second (24p) is mapped onto 60p. The first film frame (F1) becomes the first three video frames (Fr1, Fr2, Fr3). The next film frame F2 becomes the next two video frames (Fr4, Fr5). The pattern repeats.

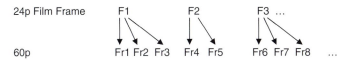

24p Film Frame

60p

FIGURE 4.5 *3:2 Pulldown Frame Rate Conversion from 24p to 60p*

Few broadcasters send 24p, even though ATSC-compliant receivers can receive and decode those formats into usable pictures. The quality impact, if this potential bandwidth savings technique were to be used in deployed receivers, is unknown.

1080 24p Opportunities

One of the few sources of 1080 24p material is from the emerging Blue Ray and HD-DVD high definition video recorders. The material is converted to the native resolution of the display. The quality of this conversion is directly dependent on the quality of the scaler. In consumer devices, the scalers are generally inexpensive and of limited computation capability. A solution is to invest in a high quality external scaler.

Broadcasters who choose to transmit in 1080 24p may be able to exploit the unused bandwidth by including eTV (covered in Chapter 7) or multicast programming. A potential multicast revenue source maybe the use of a DCC (Directed Channel Change) to extended commercial messages. Broadcasters may provide this for a fee with their ad sales packages.

Scaling is the act of spatial conversion of one pixel grid structure to another. The process increases in complexity when it involves a conversion of scanning method between interlaced and progressive. Sophisticated methods of motion compensation will correct for many of these spatial and temporal artifacts.

Conversion between pixel grids and scanning methods creates artifacts. Even though the relationship between pixels per line and the number of lines of the two HD display formats (1080 and 720) is 3 to 2, converting between formats can only be perfect when the image details are in correct ratios.

Consider a portion of a line in each format. Three consecutive pixels in the 1920 line are equivalent to two pixels in the 1280 line. The top pair of rows of Figure 4.6 shows the alignment of 1920 and 1280 pixels for each format. Notice that if the pixels on the 1920 line are divided into groups of three black pixels and three white pixels, a conversion to 1280 would produce corresponding alternating pairs of two pixels of black and white. That is, the frequency component of the bars would be maintained across the display.

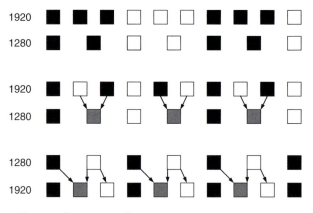

FIGURE 4.6 *Format Conversion Scenarios*

However, real world images are never so conveniently composed. There will rarely be a precise mapping of image details for the entire screen from one format to another.

Now, as shown in the second pair of rows, consider alternating black and white pixels for the 1920 line. Converting three 1920 pixels to two in a 1280 line is straight forward where pixels line up. In this instance, mapping from one format to another is exact.

But where they don't, there are choices in deciding how to convert the pixels. A method generally followed, is to average two adjacent pixels to produce the corresponding pixel in the target format. This results in gray pixels, rather than pure black or white, and a reduction in detail. Sometimes a more complicated filtering process is used. None are perfect.

Converting from 1280 to 1920 is shown in the bottom pair of rows in Figure 4.6. A similar problem exists, and when pixel averaging techniques are used, gray pixels are produced where there is not an exact alignment of pixels between formats.

Similar issues are involved when converting lines between 1080i and 720p, but now the conversion of scanning method between interlaced and progressive must be considered and is critical. Simple line doubling impacts vertical detail. Techniques like those described for pixel conversion will result in the same imperfect conversion. Figure 4.7 illustrates problems with the conversion process.

The issue is somewhat resolved when one introduces screen size and viewing distance into the perceptual equation. Image quality is subjective and these visual artifacts will diminish considerably at the proper viewing distance. The artifacts

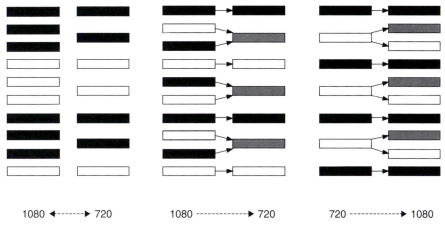

1080 ◄------► 720   1080 ------------► 720   720 ------------► 1080

FIGURE 4.7 *Format Conversion of Full Lines*

are still there, but viewing from a distance where the pixel structure disappears will reduce the aesthetically objectionable conversion errors to imperceptible.

Although engineers are concerned (and rightly so) with the numerical, mathematical and technical aspects of a video system, consumer viewing is dependent on subjective perception of the image, not on the numbers. So if the viewer is happy with the quality of their HDTV, then the format conversion process is adequate.

Aspect Ratio Interoperability

The need to display 16:9 content on 4:3 displays and vice versa will plague broadcasters until, and possibly beyond, the analog shutdown. Framing of subject matter is seriously dependent upon what the viewing aspect ratio will be. For example, if a football game is shot in 16:9 but framed for 4:3 (because it will be simulcast in both HD 16:9 and NTSC 4:3), the 4:3 image will be action packed. However, the 16:9 image will have lots of green grass behind the offensive team and much of the defensive secondary will be off the screen. Consequently, the ability to watch the entire play unfold (a receiver working his route against the defensive back while the quarterback drops back) is difficult with a 4:3 center cut.

In increasing numbers, broadcasters are electing to broadcast 16:9 HD programs letterboxed in a 4:3 SD display. However, this technique loses 120 scan lines and reduces the vertical resolution of the image.

Conversely, a program shot in 4:3 will use pillar bars to fill the 16:9 screen. Aesthetics is an issue. Neutral grey or some derivative of neighboring chrominance may be visually acceptable.

For a period of time, before HD became prevalent, an anamorphic display was somewhat acceptable. This technique either stretches a 4:3 image horizontally to 16:9 or squashes a 16:9 image into a 4:3 display. Fortunately, this technique is rarely used anymore.

The Postage Stamp Problem

A compounded aspect ratio problem arises when material traverses a distribution chain where the content is converted from one format to another and the supporting infrastructure does not take aspect ratio into account.

As an example, consider a commercial spot provided in SD. When shown on a 16:9 HD display, pillar bars will be used. But if this 16:9 feed is presented in SD, it will be a letter-boxed, pillar-barred presentation.

Figure 4.8 shows a number of postage stamp display scenarios. Image resolution is lost and the consumer does not experience their HDTV to the fullest of its capability. Less than full use of the display area causes some to feel that they have not received the maximum return on their consumer electronic investment.

This problem has been addressed by the ATSC, SMPTE and CEA and solved by use of the Active Format Descriptor (AFD). Information is contained in the transmission that describes the image format, 16:9 or 4:3. The receiver interprets this data and decides how best to format the display. Hence, when this original format

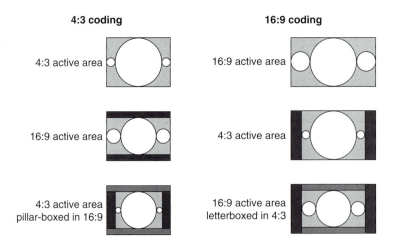

FIGURE 4.8 *Postage Stamp Scenarios, Coding and Active Area* (From A/53A, Courtesy ATSC)

information is broadcast, the postage stamp problem is resolved on all sets that support the processing of the AFD signal.

Display Color Primaries

With NTSC dependent solely on CRT display technology, there was one set of RGB color primaries. These were based on the chemical properties of materials used in displays.

Today there are numerous display technologies. LCD, DLP and others each has a slightly different chromaticity for the RGB color primaries. Hence, each display has an innate color gamut. Since the wavelength of red, green and blue will vary among display technologies, the source color will not be exactly reproduced at the receiver. Similarly, presentation of the same content on different display technologies will not be identical.

Summary

- The technology in a DTV receiver is relatively simple when compared to the amount of processing that occurs in preparing content for transmission.

- Compared to an analog television, a DTV is orders of magnitude more complex.

- In a DTV, audio, video and data packets are assembled into a program for presentation by using instructions sent in the transmission bit stream.

5 HDTV and DTV Standards

DTV is complicated. In digital systems, exact timing precision of data communication must always work perfectly. There is no room for even a one clock cycle error without introducing the potential of a glitch.

Standardization of technology and protocols allows numerous broadcast industry segments—including equipment vendors, system integrators, networks and local stations—to design and deploy equipment that will be able to interoperate with other equipment. In a sense, the standards-compliant devices speak the same language. This helps insure interoperability and reliability in multi vendor and varied technology infrastructures.

The establishment of television technical specifications is addressed by standards bodies comprised of organizations and individuals that are technical, business and creative stakeholders. Although not legally binding (with exception of standards incorporated into FCC regulations), conformance to industry standards is generally in the best interest of equipment manufactures and broadcast engineering departments.

Motivation for the creation of standards varies. Sometimes, a technical problem is to be solved. At other times, a manufacturer has built a better mouse trap and submits their technology for standardization. Or in the case of DTV in the U.S., standardization was by mandated by government decree and managed by the FCC.

Devices that follow the standards can reduce the impact of glitches or errors. Complying with standards when designing broadcast equipment and infrastructures helps insure interoperability among resources produced by various vendors.

Today, standards organizations are taking a proactive role. Representatives from vendors, broadcasters and other stakeholders are forming working groups to address emerging needs during the transition to digital infrastructures for new workflows, processes and equipment.

Standards Bodies

Many standards bodies are defining the technology of DTV. Active organizations in the United States that establish relevant digital television production, transmission and consumer electronics standards include:

- Advanced Television Systems Committee (ATSC)

- Society of Motion Picture and Television Engineers (SMPTE)

- Audio Engineering Society (AES)

- Society of Cable Telecommunication Engineers (SCTE)

- Consumer Electronics Association (CEA)

- Institute of Electrical and Electronic Engineers (IEEE)

The scope of various standards bodies is illustrated in Figure 5.1 with respect to their role in the production, broadcast and consumption of televised content.

Digital television was standardized by the ATSC based on the working prototype developed by the Grand Alliance. Dolby's AC-3, now known as Dolby Digital, though not a Grand Alliance member, was documented as the ATSC's digital audio standard and is also included in the DVB standards. The portions of these standards that have been adopted by the FCC carry the weight of regulation.

Other DTV standards are voluntary. Production-related standards for the television and film industries are developed and ratified by the SMPTE. Audio standards are developed by the Audio Engineering Society (AES). Both the SMPTE and the AES are international standards bodies.

Completing the media chain, the CEA address consumer technology standards. Antenna performance, receiver specifications and closed captioning are among standardized technologies.

The Institute of Electrical and Electronic Engineers (IEEE) includes a Broadcast Technology Society (BTS) that has historically focused on radio frequency transmission and display engineering. But with file-based networked production infrastructures,

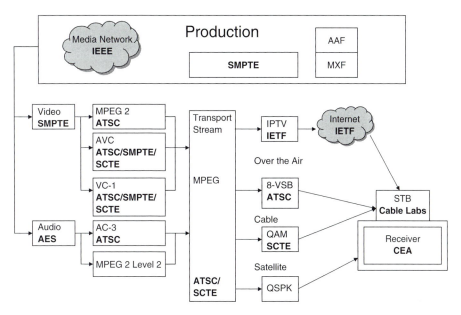

FIGURE 5.1 *Standards Bodies for U.S. DTV*

nontraditional broadcast engineering disciplines such as IEEE LAN and computer imaging are now relevant to the media industry.

American National Standards Institute (ANSI)

The American National Standards Institute (ANSI) coordinates the development and use of voluntary consensus standards in the U. S. and represents the needs and views of U.S. stakeholders in standardization forums around the globe. Founded in 1918, it mission is "to enhance both the global competitiveness of U.S. business and the U.S. quality of life by promoting and facilitating voluntary consensus standards and conformity assessment systems, and safeguarding their integrity."

The Institute is the U.S. representative to the two major non-treaty international standards organizations, the International Organization for Standardization (ISO), and, via the U.S. National Committee (USNC), the International Electrotechnical Commission (IEC).

Through ANSI, the U.S. has access to the ISO and IEC standards development processes. ANSI participates in the technical programs of both the ISO and the IEC and administers many committees and subgroups. Part of its responsibilities as the U.S. member body to the ISO include accrediting U.S. Technical Advisory Groups (U.S. TAGs), whose primary purpose is to develop and transmit, via ANSI, U.S. positions on activities and ballots of the international technical committee. U.S. positions for the IEC are endorsed and closely monitored by the USNC Technical Management Committee (TMC).

The ANSI Board of Standards Review (BSR) approves standards as American National Standards (ANS). ANSI BSR approval of a standard as an ANS is based on procedural compliance, i.e., the process by which the technical content was developed. The ANSI BSR evaluates whether technical issues were afforded due process in accordance with ANSI's requirements and the ANSI-accredited standards developer's procedures. Most standards organizations follow the ANSI due process requirements to a large degree, whether or not they are ANSI Accredited.

The procedures that govern the American National Standards process are called the ANSI Essential Requirements: Due process requirements for American National Standards (ANSI Essential Requirements).

These include:

- consensus must be reached on a proposed standard by a group or "consensus body" that includes representatives from all stakeholders

- draft standards must undergo open public reviews, and any member of the public may submit comments

- comments must be evaluated, responded to and if appropriate, incorporated into the draft standard

- anyone believing that due process principles were not sufficiently respected during the standards development process has the right to appeal

Working Groups (WG) are formed after a proposal for development or ratification or a technology or process is submitted. Generally, the topic will fall under the auspices of an existing working group. Otherwise an Ad-Hoc WG will be formed. A project plan is developed and ultimately leads to a draft document.

Technology Integration

With the transition to digital broadcasting, content delivery over numerous transmission channels and the development of IT based broadcast systems, many previously uninvolved standards bodies now influence DTV. Standards bodies are incorporating and referencing other protocols traditionally not within their scope. This is a result of technology integration in media systems and the marriage of broadcast engineering and information technology. In the consumer domain this is blurring of lines of demarcation between the TV and PC.

For example, the IETF (Internet Engineering Task Force) recently issued RFC 4539 "Media Type Registration for the SMPTE Material Exchange Format." SMPTE has issued a candidate for MPEG Transport Stream packets over IP networks. A decade ago, this would have been unimaginable.

Another example is the action by Microsoft to present the Windows Media Video compression algorithm to SMPTE and the ATSC for ratification as a video compression methodology. The impact of this is that source code is now released. The algorithm has been slightly altered and renamed VC-1.

International Standards Bodies

An initial, albeit lofty, goal of early HDTV standardization efforts was to develop a global production standard. Many U.S. DTV standards have been influenced by and incorporate work undertaken by international standards bodies.

DTV-relevant international organizations include:

- Digital Video Broadcasting (DVB)
- International Telecommunications Union (ITU)
- International Standards Organization (ISO)
- European Broadcasting Union (EBU)
- European Television Standards Institute (ETSI)

It is the coordination of efforts among these various organizations that has led to the emerging global deployment of DTV. Compared to the NTSC/PAL/SECAM divergence of analog color TV, the implementation of MPEG and a layered system has led to many similarities in global DTV standards. In fact, 1080 24p has become a global production standard used by the television and film industries, since it can easily be transcoded into other video formats.

An Interdependent, Layered Approach

A toolkit approach is used by many standardized technology methodologies. The idea is that features can be used or omitted if desired, and modules can be mixed and matched for a particular design requirement. On a larger scale, conceptualized interchangeable layers can be used in complicated multi-technology systems to facilitate flexible design. The ATSC DTV system utilizes this layered approach. So do other MPEG based systems such as DVB.

As described in Chapter 3, the flexibility of modular DTV standards has allowed cable and satellite transmission using forms of digital modulation other than the

8-VSB used by the ATSC system. The benefit is that DTV receivers need only have an adaptable multi-format demodulation front end while the other subsystems are consistent with the ATSC presentation, compression and transport layers.

DVB has opted for a completely different transmission technology. Coded Orthogonal Frequency Division Multiplex (COFDM) was so successful in the DVB implementation that it was touted as an alternative when early DTV receivers were not able to work where expected.

Standards ratified by one organization often incorporate standards developed by other organizations. There are two methods of reference. A normative reference is a used as a foundation, portions of which can be considered part of a standard. An informative reference is intended to aid in understanding a standard and need not be implemented to comply with the standard.

For example, the ATSC ACAP Standard A/101 incorporates portions of 58 normative references! An additional four informative references are listed as well.

Another important consideration is the precise definition of how terms are used in the document. As a wider range of standards bodies are involved in digital media, misunderstandings are more likely because the same terms are used differently by the television or computing technical communities.

Standards Document Format

Documents produced by the standards organizations follow a general format and include many of the following sections.

- Abstract: general description of the nature of the document and why it is needed

- Introduction: describes the role of standard body that developed this document

- Scope: what this standard addresses and what it does not cover

- References: normative and informative documents included by reference

- Definition of terms: precise definition as used in the context of this document

- Tech details: details of technologies and processes

- Appendices: examples and additional information

- Annexes: enhancements that are compatible with the standard

Standards and Intellectual Property Rights

Standards sometimes incorporate patented technology. This is a motivating factor for organizations to develop and submit patented technology and processes for standardization. Many standards documents now have a notice regarding that use of intellectual property may be necessary to adhere to the standard.

MPEG is an example of how a complicated standard, with many organizations holding IP rights, is administered. Known as the MPEG Licensing Authority (MPEG LA), it is not related to any standards setting body but is an independent administrative service that enables one-stop licensing for patents incorporated into the MPEG standard.

The LA enables MPEG-2 users to acquire patent rights from multiple patent holders in a single transaction as an alternative to negotiating separate licenses. MPEG LA currently administers MPEG-2, MPEG-2 Systems, MPEG 4 Visual, MPEG 4 Systems, IEEE 1394, DVB-T and AVC/H.264 Intellectual Property rights. It is developing rights administration programs for DRM, VC-1, ATSC, DVB-H and Blue Ray Disk technologies.

The ATSC Standards

The development of HD and DTV standards has never really reached an end. Existing standards continue to evolve, while new candidate standards undergo the formal ratification process as new media technologies emerge.

It is only natural to begin with the Advanced Television Systems Committee DTV standard. This technology represents more than a decade of R & D and prototype development.

Over time, both the scope and number of ATSC standards have grown. Documents now include Recommended Practices, Implementation Subcommittee Findings, and Technology Group Reports.

Initially, the ATSC was tasked with documenting the "winning" system during the competitive phase of HDTV proponent testing. Today the ATSC has continued as the DTV standards development body for 8-VSB related DTV (in all its flavors). Candidate Standards are regularly proposed.

Modularity of the ATSC system allows for the new and improved compression algorithms, such as the MPEG-4 Part 10 based Advanced Video Coding (AVC), to be seamlessly substituted for MPEG-2. ATSC has issued Candidate Standards for coding constraints and transport of AVC. Of course, to use one of these, the receiver needs to have an AVC-capable decoder.

The toolkit approach offers design choices. Frame rate, raster, refresh rate and scanning methods can be combined in a number of ways. Compression options include I, P or B frame; bit rate; and GOP structure. The transport mechanism facilitates either single or multiple programs along with data services.

The original DTV standard was described in two ATSC documents, A/52: "Digital Audio Compression (AC-3) Standard" and A/53: "ATSC Digital Television Standard". A companion publication, A/54: "Guide to the ATSC Digital Television Standard" provides tutorial information, an overview of the digital television system and recommendations for operating parameters for certain aspects of the DTV system. For more information on specific standards, visit www.atsc.org.

A/53 ATSC Digital Television Standard

All the decades of work to develop digital high definition television culminated in the A/53 standard. For all this effort and expense, 133 pages were produced. This was sufficient to launch DTV in the U.S.

A/53E, the "ATSC Digital Television Standard, Revision E with Amendment No. 1 and 2" defines the system characteristics of the advanced television (ATV) system. Detailed specifications of the system include:

- video encoder input scanning formats and the pre-processing and compression parameters of the video encoder

- the audio encoder input signal format and the pre-processing and compression parameters of the audio encoder (actually specified in A/52 and included as an informative reference in A/53)

- the service multiplex and transport layer characteristics

- the VSB RF/Transmission subsystem

The system is modular in concept and the specifications for each of the modules are provided in the appropriate annex.

Video Presentation

Ultimately, one of 18 ATSC video formats must be compressed. The formats are comprised of combinations of four attributes: aspect ratio, raster format, scanning methodology and frame repetition rate. This will be HD at 1080i or 720p, or SD at

VERTICAL LINES	PIXELS	ASPECT RATIO	PICTURE RATE
1080	1920	16:9	60i, 30p, 24p
720	1280	16:9	60p, 30p, 24p
480	704	16:9 and 4:3	60p, 60i, 30p, 24p
480	640	4:3	60p, 60i, 30p, 24p

TABLE 5.1 *Digital Television Standard Video Formats* (From A/54A, Courtesy ATSC)

480p or 480i. The use of various color space sampling structures further complicates the definition of formats.

Most notably, the FCC declined to adopt the set of formats in the version of the ATSC recommended standard, so there are no definitions of scanning formats in the FCC rules. This has led to a logo certification program, but decoding of all 18 formats is not required by law. Therefore any MPEG-2 Main Profile at High Level video format that also complies with the other constraints in the ATSC standard can be sent as the one required video service.

Video Compression

The ATSC limits the presentation formats and refers to them as MPEG Compression restraints, as shown in Table 5.1. This is the infamous "Table 3" that led to a year delay in the adoption of the ATSC standard by the FCC.

> Traditionally, broadcast standards have been specified in the language of engineering mathematics. With the transition to digital technology, portions of the ATSC and other standards such as AC-3 and MPEG are specified in a manner similar to the C programming language.

ATSC Transport Streams

An ATSC transport stream is a 19.39 Mbps, one-way, digital data pipe from the program originator to a viewer. In addition to audio and video, any type of data that can be decoded by an HDTV receiver or set top box can be delivered to enhance the media consumer's experience.

Therefore, a broadcast infrastructure must now support more than audio, video and graphics. Data services, such as program guides and interactive features, necessitate expanded implementations of IT technologies in a digital BOC.

The realization that the 19.39 Mbps Grand Alliance transport stream (TS) could carry multiple SD programs came late in the process. This did not please some in Congress, however the FCC explicitly touted the extra capability and only required a DTV service equal to or greater than NTSC quality. The perception that the replacement DTV service on the second 6 MHz channel would be a stimulus to simulcast HD transmission was shattered.

From its conception, the ATSC transport stream was always intended to deliver more than 5.1 audio and HDTV video. Even the earliest TS specifications included a program guide methodology. Many of the ATSC standards are devoted to TS-delivered data services.

Building Transport Packets

Compression engines produce audio and video Elementary Streams (ES) which are then encapsulated into Packetized Elementary Streams (PES). Each PES packet consists of a PES packet start code, PES header flags, PES packet header fields and a payload. A PES packet can be up to 65,536 bytes in length.

Each PES packet is assigned a Packet ID (PID) common to the ES from which it was derived. PES packets are divided and placed into Transport Packets, usually before they leave the compression equipment.

As discussed in Chapter 3, transport packet consists of 188 bytes. The first byte of the four-byte packet header is the sync byte and has the hex value of 0×47. The Packet ID, a 13-bit value, is used to uniquely mark each audio, video or data ES. A four-bit Continuity Counter field allows verification that packets have not been dropped. The remaining bits signal PES start, transport error and priority, scrambling and whether an optional adaptation field is present.

Ultimately, transport packets are multiplexed into a constant 19.39 Mbps ATSC transport stream for over-the-air delivery of HDTV. The bit rate cannot be larger. Add something and something else must be removed. Figure 5.2 illustrates the structure of an ATSC transport stream.

A single program (SPTS) or multiple programs (MPTS) may be carried in a transport stream. PID values are the key to assembling individual programs from an MPTS. It is this capability that enables multicasting.

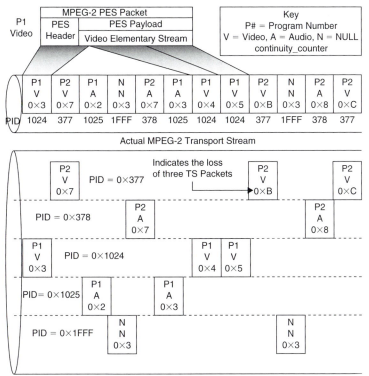

FIGURE 5.2 *MPEG-2 Transport Stream Program Multiplex* (From A/53E, Courtesy ATSC)

Assembling a Program: TS Multiplex

Originally, the ATSC used MPEG Program and System Information (PSI) methodologies to describe to the receiver the contents of the TS and what elements to assemble into a program. A method for supplying program guide information was also specified. These were documented in A/55 and A/56.

The two methods were combined and modified and have now evolved to become the standardization of Program and System Information Protocol (PSIP) as documented in ATSC A/65C.

ATSC Transmission

VSB modulation, developed for the GA by Zenith, has been the target of much debate since the adoption of the ATSC standard in 1996. Subsequent generations of VSB

storage of audio on magnetic, optical, semiconductor, or other storage media. Revision B added a new annex, "Enhanced AC-3 Bit Stream Syntax" which specifies an additional syntax that offers additional coding tools and features, including additional channels of audio beyond the original 5.1.

AC-3 Metadata

Consistency of volume levels and production quality must be maintained through all segments of a broadcast. The FCC has allowed broadcasters to self-police the use of AC-3 metadata to maintain consistent volume levels between programs and commercials. Besides, now that many viewers have home theatre sound systems, audio presentation has become an aesthetic issue.

Three AC-3 Metadata parameters can be set during production to insure consistent audio presentation.

- Dialnorm is a number that describes the relative volume of a program. It is intended to maintain a constant audio level regardless of source material. When properly implemented, it can mitigate the annoying problem of a commercial being louder than the program.

- Dynamic range is user-adjustable. It allows setting of maximum and minimum volume levels. So for a football game you may want to have the widest range possible, yet late at night, lowering the peak volumes will insure your wife and kids can remain asleep while you watch a rock concert!

- Down-mixing signals the mixer as to the format of the audio so that a suitable mix for stereo can be created. Not all DTV consumers will have 5.1 systems, so down-mixing adapts the signal to the consumer's system.

A/65: Program and System Information Protocol

A major concern of broadcasters that must transition to DTV and move transmission operations over to their replacement (temporarily the second) "DTV" channel is maintaining brand image and channel number association. Many viewers think in terms of a channel number ("Channel 2") rather than by network affiliation or local call letters. Stations have invested considerable sums in getting this numerical branding message to their audience. It was considered important to carry this (often subconscious) association into the DTV era and maintain this analog channel brand association, even after the NTSC shutdown.

The MPEG-2 Systems standard did not address three issues important DTV in the U.S. These were:

- Naming: use of call letters or other friendly terminology

- Numbers: assignment of channel numbers independent of the RF channel number (as had been done with analog TV)

- Navigation: delivery of data to electronic programming guides that could display the current and future program schedule

The Solution PSIP: TS Metadata

Replacing the original ATSC System Information for Digital Television (A/56) standard and the Program Guide for Digital Television (A/55) (both now withdrawn), the Program and System Information Protocol (PSIP) standard, A/65B, defines tables that describe elements of a DTV service present in a transport stream. PSIP enables demultiplexing of packets from the TS such that a programming "event" is reconstructed and presented. PSIP is implemented as MPEG Syntax Private data. It also enables predicted video and audio PID selection by the receiver to reduce channel change time. It has been totally incorporated into the FCC regulations.

A/65C, the "Program and System Information Protocol for Terrestrial Broadcast and Cable, Rev. C, with Amendment No. 1" defines the standard protocol for transmission of the relevant data tables contained within packets carried in the transport stream multiplex required for program assembly.

A Recommended Practice (A/69: Program and System Information Protocol Implementation Guidelines for Broadcasters) is available. It provides a set of guidelines for the use and implementation of PSIP

PSIP introduces the concept of "virtual" channel, where the channel number is not tied to the RF carrier frequency. An opportunity presented by DTV is not only the ability to broadcast HDTV but also to transmit a "multicast" of any number of digital services. As compression efficiency improves, more services or a higher quality can be supported at the broadcasters' option.

Channel Number

PSIP requires the broadcaster/channel number relationship to continue by designating major and minor numbers for each broadcast service. The major number is identical to the NTSC analog channel number. PSIP information can link the new radio frequency channel to the analog channel number.

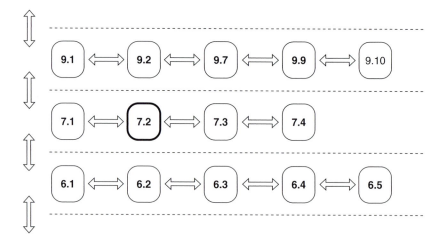

FIGURE 5.4 *Two-Dimensional Channel Navigation Using Major and Minor Numbers to find 7.2* (From A/69, Courtesy ATSC)

Naming conventions follow a "Major.Minor" convention. So if "Channel 4" NSTC is now sending DTV on RF channel 47, the virtual channel number displayed will always have a major number of 4. The analog RF channel licensed to each station is the permanently assigned major number (both in the standard and by FCC regulation) for each NTSC station. The first digital channel will be 4.1 followed by 4.2, 4.3 etc. Any one of these channels may be HD or SD, though many broadcasters tend to use the first minor channel (.1) for HD. There are detailed rules for special assignment of the major numbers in Annex B of A/65 to cover simulcast and stations that are granted licenses in the future. The DTV signal can also announce the contents of the NTSC channel by using 'zero' as the minor number, 4.0 in this example. Minor numbers greater than 99 denote data services.

Figure 5.4 illustrates how the Major.Minor channel numbers are used for channel navigation. All services associated with a broadcaster's NTSC channel number are the major number. A "0" Minor number is reserved for the NTSC channel. Minor channel numbers from "1" and above are assigned to each digital program service.

Virtual Channels

PSIP uses a relational or "pointers" methodology. Various tables contain linked information that allows for flexibility. Base tables, all transported in packets with a PID of 0x1FFB provide the necessary information to find and decode available channels. Base tables consist of the Virtual Channel Table (VCT), Regional Rating Table (RRT) if sent, Master Guide Table (MGT) and System Time Table (SST). (See Figure 5.6)

Major num.	Minor num.	Short name	Carrier freq. (MHz)	Channel TSID	Progr. num.	Flags	Service type	Source id	Descriptors
12	0	NBZ	205.25	0×0AA0	0×FFFF	--	analog	12	ch_name
12	1	NBZD	620.31	0×0AA1	0×0001	--	digital	1	ch_name serv_locat.
12	2	NBZ-S	620.31	0×0AA1	0×0002	--	digital	2	ch_name serv_locat.
12	3	NBZ-M	620.31	0×0AA1	0×0003	--	digital	3	ch_name serv_locat.
12	4	NBZ-H	620.31	0×0AA1	0×0004	--	digital	4	ch_name serv_locat.

FIGURE 5.5 *Content of the Virtual Channel Table* (From A/65C, Courtesy ATSC)

The Master Guide Table describes all other tables, their PIDs and size. The Virtual Channel Table (VCT) has the list of services, and the System Time Table (STT) has the number of seconds since midnight January 6, 1980 with respect to UTC.

Figure 5.5 shows the VCT entries for a Major channel number 12. As can be seen, the minor number enables tuning to the desired program by indicating the carrier frequency. Programs are called "events" in PSIP-DTV speak.

Parental control is enabled via the content advisory descriptor in the EIT. The content advisory descriptor is used to apply these labels to content. The descriptor uses RRT table value of 0 × 01 for the U.S. and U.S. possessions. Sending the RRT itself is optional in the U.S. The meanings of the values in RRT 0 × 01 are defined in CEA-766-B, along with constraints on the allowed combinations. Canada's RRT has been assigned value 0 × 02.

Electronic Program Guide

Information that can be used by Electronic Program Guides (EPG) is delivered in PSIP data. The Event Information Table (EIT) is spilt into three-hour blocks of the schedule, and transmitted as separate sub-tables. EIT-0 is the current table, EIT-1 is the three hour plus, and so on. UTC times are used in the EIT. In the Report and Order, the FCC specifically affirmed its adoption of the standard's minimum requirement to

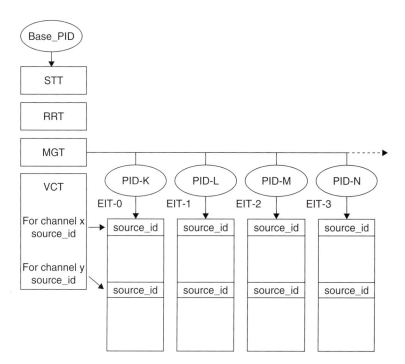

FIGURE 5.6 *The Table Hierarchy for the Program and System Information Protocol* (From A/65C, Courtesy ATSC)

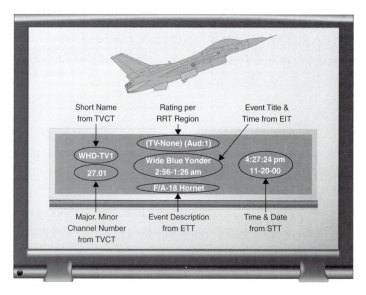

FIGURE 5.7 *EPG information display and the corresponding PSIP tables* (After A/69, Courtesy ATSC)

always send the first four three-hour time segments (EIT-0 through 3). There is a 14-bit event ID, which uniquely identifies an event when it is used in conjunction with the source ID (one for each virtual channel).

The optional Extended Text Table (ETT) contains the locations of Extended Text Messages (ETM). An ETM_location field points to additional text info about an event. These entries support multiple languages.

By using EIT, sometimes supplemented by ETT information, an EPG can be assembled and displayed on a receiver as shown in Figure 5.7. Advanced EPG features may include automated program recording at the push of a dedicated remote control button.

ATSC Data Services

As the broadcast industry moves into a multi-format, cross-platform media methodology, ATSC transport stream standards have expanded to define algorithms that facilitate data delivery. Transport stream extensions are the enabling methodology to implement an enhanced HDTV experience. Data delivery standards, equipment and authoring applications are being developed for creation and transmission of these data dependent services.

Enjoyment of watching a broadcast is sometimes impeded by crawls, bugs and other superimposed graphics or animations. Years ago, they were interesting differentiating features, but now they frequently divert attention away from the program. Wouldn't it be wonderful to control what can be seen on the screen, or ask for more info, purchase an item or see an extended commercial? ATSC data capabilities can make this a reality.

Flow Down Stream

Transport stream data delivery facilitates applications such as enhanced television, Webcasting and streaming video services. Interoperable standards will make this technology transparent to the viewer, easy to use, reliable and secure. They are the enabling technologies of what is envisioned as the media networked home of tomorrow.

The foundation of all data delivery standards is the ATSC Standard A/90 Data Broadcast Standard. It defines protocols for download of data and delivery of datagrams compatible with digital multiplex transport streams. The standard supports data services that are both program-related and non-program-related. A/91, "Implementation Guidelines for the Data Broadcast Standard," provides a set of guidelines for the use and implementation of ATSC A/90 Data Broadcast Standard.

ATSC working and study groups have recommended additional standards using A/90 as their basis. Many have been adopted. Together, this suite of specifications enables interoperability among applications by providing a common protocol.

Software updates or upgrades of firmware, operating system software and device driver software can be accomplished via TS data. A/94, the "ATSC Data Application Reference Model," defines an Application Reference Model (ARM). A/95, "Transport Stream File System Standard (TSFS)," defines the standard for delivery of directories and files, and A/97,"Software Download Data Service," specifies a data service that may be used to download software. The content and format of the software download data is not defined by this standard. The formats and interpretations of the software download payload are defined by each user of this standard.

Completing the interactive suite, A/93, "Synchronized/Asynchronous Trigger Standard," facilitates transmission of data elements and events to a DTV data services capable receiver. A/96, "ATSC Interaction Channel Protocols," defines a core suite of protocols to enable remote interactivity in television environments.

Upstream Communication: The Back Channel

Killer apps are hunted like treasure, and the killer app of HDTV may be interactive TV (iTV). Precisely speaking, iTV is really a capability-enabling technology, while the actual features the standards facilitate are the real "killer apps." Examples of remote interactivity include e-commerce transactions during commercials, electronic banking, polling and e-mail services.

Interactivity requires the use of a two-way channel that enables communication between the client device and remote servers, the "back channel." The back channel scenario differs for each content delivery channel. OTA transmission lacks a RF back channel, but ATSC has adopted a standard for data that flows over an arbitrary physical means (A/96). DBS also suffers from lack of a back channel. Cable systems have a "built-in" back channel.

The Common Data Receiver

Interactive and enhanced applications need access to common receiver features in a platform-independent manner. Adopted in 2002, A/100, "DTV Application Software Environment—Level 1 (DASE-1)," defines middleware that permits programming content and applications to run uniformly on all brands and models of receivers. The fundamental concepts it employed are illustrative of how data services are implemented.

DASE video layers represent different kinds of content to be presented. Figure 5.8 shows how these layers are assembled on a display. Alpha channels can be

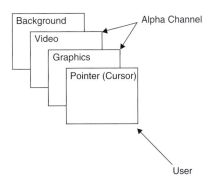

FIGURE 5.8 *DASE Conceptual Display Model* (From A/100-1, Courtesy ATSC)

opaque or transparent. This layered approach, along with transport stream signaling, allows backward compatibility with DTV receivers that do not have data reception capabilities.

Frequently, by the time a technology gets through the standardization process, an improvement has come along. Similarly, in less than three years, DASE and OCAP[1] are now the basis of a proposed new ATSC standard that enables interactive features. The "Advanced Common Applications Platform (ACAP)" specification (A/101) seeks to ensure interoperability between ACAP applications and different implementations of platforms supporting ACAP. The ACAP standard is intended to apply to broadcast systems and receivers for OTA broadcast and cable TV systems but may also be applied to other transport systems such as satellite. ATSC recently approved A/102, which defines how to announce ACAP services using PSIP data structures.

Will DTV Data Services Replace the Internet?

Eventually, the Internet will be fully integrated with every device in a home media network. A/92, "Delivery of IP Multicast Sessions over Data Broadcast" specifies the delivery of Internet Protocol (IP) multicast sessions, the delivery of data for describing the characteristics of a session, and usage of the ATSC A/90 Data Broadcast Standard for IP Multicast. Use of the Session Description Protocol (SDP) is an integral part of the IP Multicast-based data broadcast service.

This is the first step in getting a DTV receiver connected to the Web. Addition of a back channel will complete the implementation. The convergence of the television and personal computer is being facilitated by the ATSC data services standards.

---

1. OCAP has continued to evolve and new versions have been adopted by the SCTE as SCTE 90-1.

SMPTE Standards

The Society of Motion Picture and Television Engineers, generally referred to as "the SMPTE," develops ANSI-approved voluntary standards, recommended practices, and engineering guidelines addressing production processes. SMPTE also develops test materials providing a common denominator for design, implementation and calibration of broadcast engineering systems.

SMPTE was founded in 1916 to advance theory and development in the motion imaging field. The organization is international in scope with headquarters in White Plains, New York, and chapters in the U.S., England, Australia and other nations around the world.

In addition to developing industry standards SMPTE is active in enhancing member education through seminars, exhibitions and conferences, communicating the latest developments in technology and promoting networking and interaction.

With the migration to Digital Intermediary by the film industry and the emergence of 1080 24 fps as a global production standard, SMPTE's involvement in both period film and television is becoming increasingly important. Distinctions between the two mediums are fading. Some films are now "shot" as digital video and "conformed" to a "film look," while others are shot on film and converted to an HD format for broadcast. Hence, coordination of production and technical standards is becoming a necessity for efficient content exchange and repurposing.

SMPTE Digital Television Standards

The use of digital technology in television production goes back to the 1980s. CCIR 601 defined digital video characteristics. SMPTE 259 followed quickly on and standardized the Serial Digital Interface (SDI). Serial data has the advantage of being carried on one wire instead of 9-, 15- or 25-pin DB connectors.

SMPTE's involvement with HD standards began with the controversial ratification of the NHK-proposed 1125 analog HD format as SMPTE 240M. A landmark effort was the work of the Joint EBU/SMPTE Task Force for Harmonized Standards for the Exchange of Program Material as Bit Streams. A major forward-looking effort that culminated in two documents, the group's charter was to guide the development of standards relevant to the implementation of bit stream based television systems.

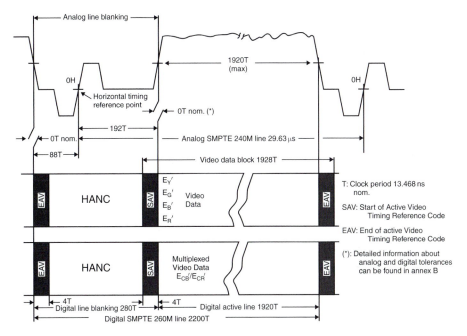

FIGURE 5.9 *Analog SMPTE 240M and Digital SMPTE 260M Video Line Comparison* (After SMPTE 260M, Courtesy SMPTE)

Television Formats

Submission of the analog HDTV production specification by NHK in the 1980s and what ultimately became SMPTE240 can be cited as the dawn of the HD standardization process. With the advent of all-digital technologies SMPTE 240 has been retired. But it is useful as a point of reference in comparing the differences between analog and digital television.

SMPTE 240 defined the analog while SMPTE 260M the digital implementations of 1125-line HDTV production systems. Figure 5.9 illustrates the conceptual differences between analog and digital line signals.

SMPTE 274M-2005 and 296M-2001 define a family of HD raster-scanning systems for the representation of stationary or moving two-dimensional images sampled temporally at a constant frame rate and having image formats of 1920×1080 and 1280×720 with an aspect ratio of 16:9.

Analog video and the bit-parallel digital interface is, for all intents and purposes, replaced by the Serial Digital Interface (SDI) specified in SMPTE 259 for SD and SMPTE 292 for HD.

Compression

With the evolution to file-based production, SMPTE's scope has expanded to encompass compression methodology. Early work included low compression ratio (lossless) standards for digital tape storage systems. More recently, high compression ratio (lossy) systems have been considered.

The first such was based on Microsoft's Windows Media Video compression algorithm, which became SMPTE 421. Notably, the compression algorithm is not specified in this standard. Both progressive and interlaced video formats are supported by VC-1 include.

Serial Data Interface

Data transfer speed is an important issue in digital system design. Communication of bytes and words attains maximum speed if all 8 or 16 bits are transferred at the same moment in time (in one synchronous clock cycle). To do this, 8 or 16 distinct "traces" on a printed circuit board or wires in a cable must be utilized.

In file-based networked environments, IT has moved towards a one cable, serial data transfer methodology. The challenge is that moving eight bits serially over the same time period takes eight times the "clock" speed of a moving the data over a parallel 8-bit bus.

With the advancement of technologies that facilitate moving away from parallel data transmission to serial interfaces, so too have the early digital video parallel interfaces been defined in serial implementations.

Figure 5.10 illustrates the characteristics of parallel and serial data transfer and conversion from one to the other. An important concept is that data is valid only on a system clock edge and that the serial clock is a multiple of the parallel data clock for a parallel to serial conversion. In Figure 5.10, the serial clock is four times the parallel clock. This multiple is the number of bits that will be converted.

Serial distribution of SD and HD is ubiquitous in a modern facility. Analog RGB and composite have practically disappeared from networks and large stations. SD and HD SMPTE Serial Digital Interface (SDI) standards specify data format for real time signal distribution.

Separate standards are defined to accommodate the different data rates of uncompressed SD and HD. SMPTE 259 defines serial bit streams of 143, 270 and 360 Mbps. HD is defined in SMPTE 292 at a 1.485 Gbps. Since these are real-time signals, they possess many of the characteristics of analog video in a digital representation.

Markers signal the Start of Active Video (SAV) and End of Active Video (EAV), which result in horizontal and vertical blanking intervals where there is no active

Parallel to Serial

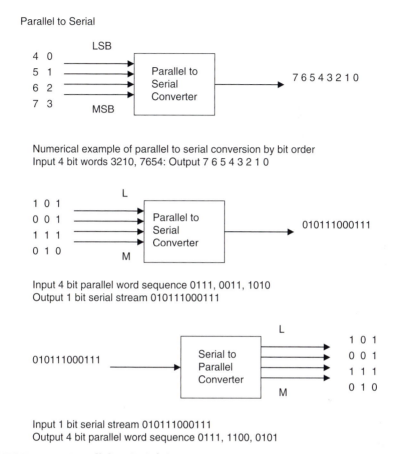

Numerical example of parallel to serial conversion by bit order
Input 4 bit words 3210, 7654: Output 7 6 5 4 3 2 1 0

Input 4 bit parallel word sequence 0111, 0011, 1010
Output 1 bit serial stream 010111000111

Input 1 bit serial stream 010111000111
Output 4 bit parallel word sequence 0111, 1100, 0101

FIGURE 5.10 *Parallel to Serial Conversion*

video data present. (See Figure 5.9.) These areas are used to convey ancillary data such as audio, closed captions, test signals, control metadata and other evolving application specific information.

For HD SMPTE 292 signals, coaxial cable interfaces are suitable where the signal loss does not exceed an amount specified by the receiver manufacturer. Typical loss amounts would be in the range of up to 20 dB at one-half the clock frequency. Fiber optic interfaces are suitable for application at up to 2 km of distance using single-mode fiber.

Ancillary Data

In the area not used for video or sync data in an SDI stream, the opportunity exists to insert data packets. This ancillary data can be in the vertical (VANC) or horizontal

(HANC) blanking intervals. This methodology can be applied to 525-line, 625-line, component or composite, and high-definition digital television interfaces which provide 8- or 10-bit data ancillary data space. As the bit rate for the potentially very large set of ancillary data packets is highly variable and the degree of support changes with time, the space used in each VANC/HANC (effectively bit-rate supported) is defined for each connecting interface.

Use of ancillary data capabilities is being investigated for facility distribution of machine control metadata. The goal is to streamline the production process and reduce system configuration and operational tasks and errors. An area of particular concern is the automation of PSIP information generation from the many systems needed to produce this information in a timely, efficient manner.

Serial Data Transport

An SDI stream can also be used to distribute raw digital data. However, because of the use of 0 × 000 and 0 × 3FF as SAV, EAV markers, these values are prohibited for use elsewhere in the SDI stream. A method has been devised to avoid synchronization problems that may arrive when these values appear in a data stream carried over SDI.

There are three serial data standards that are in widespread use. SMPTE 305M-2005, "Serial Data Transport Interface," specifies a data stream protocol used to transport packetized data compatible with 10-bit operation of SMPTE 259M (SDI). Ancillary data packets (metadata) defined by SMPTE 291M in the horizontal blanking interval (HANC) are used to identify the payload application.

SMPTE 310M-2004 specifies a "Synchronous Serial Interface for MPEG-2 Digital Transport Stream." It describes the physical interface and modulation characteristics for a synchronous serial interface to carry MPEG-2 transport bit streams at rates up to 40 Mbp/s. The standard is employed as a signal interface with transmission equipment.

Enabling the transport of various formats of video files, SMPTE 326M-2000, "SDTI Content Package Format (SDTI-CP)," specifies the format for the transport of content packages (CP) over the serial digital transport interface (SDTI). This includes all audio and video elements and metadata formats. (Chapter 6 discusses the relationship of content packages, audio, video and metadata.)

SMPTE Test Signals and Specifications

SMPTE provides guidelines on methods for aligning and testing device and system performance. Test materials are also available.

SMPTE Test Materials

SMPTE Test Materials are made in accordance with SMPTE recommendations and practices. They are important in that they are a common, independent source of technical tools used to verify system performance across industry equipment. The available materials include:

- video cassette for receiver/monitor setup

- subjective color reference films/slides

- operational alignment test films

- alignment and resolution test films

- operational registration test films

- mid-frequency response test films

- safe action and safe title area test films

SMPTE also offers VC-1 Test Materials under license including bitstreams and a reference decoder.

Testing System Colorimetry

Calibration of image capture and display color primaries are precisely defined. The familiar color bar test signal enables system alignment. RP 219-2002: High-Definition, Standard-Definition Compatible Color Bar Signal includes specification of a color bar pattern compatible with both HD and SD environments. The multi-format color bar signal is originated as an HDTV signal with an aspect ratio of 16:9 and may be down-converted to an SDTV color bar signal with an aspect ratio of either 4:3 or 16:9.

Precise voltages are defined for analog systems. Digital systems have numerical values for each primary and YUV levels corresponding to each color in the color bar test pattern.

Color Space Conversion

NTSC as well as SD and HD DTV systems have taken into account the gamut and color capabilities of display technologies. Color space conversion between analog, SD and HD, and digital systems is necessary. Each uses different RGB to/from YUV color space conversion matrix coefficients. Problems can also arise from the generation of illegal colors, often produced by compositing computer graphics on video or conversion between SD and HD content.

EG 36-2000, "Transformation Between Television Component Color Signals," describes the derivation of the transformation matrices and lists example transformations between color component signals, adopting ITU-R BT.601 and ITU-R BT.709 luma/chroma equations for both the digital and analog component signal sets.

Display Alignment

When producing content and graphics for an HD/SD simulcast, the issue of aspect ratio compatibility is important. RP 187 defines active video with respect to synchronization pulses, while RP 218 specifies a "safe title" production area for content display.

Synchronization

Alignment of horizontal and vertical synchronization pulses with respect to digital video must be precise, to the exact pixel and line. This timing must be maintained through the entire production infrastructure. RP 187 guides engineers and technicians through this alignment procedure, defining picture center and aspect ratio for a number of existing video standards, and providing a technique that may be used to define center and aspect ratio for future standards.

The document is intended to be used for calibration of image generation and display devices. It is also intended as a reference for designers of such equipment (particularly graphics devices), and for designers of processing equipment such as image-manipulation devices.

Safe Title

Not all receivers reproduce the picture exactly as is was captured at the source. Over-scanning is frequently used to insure that the image fills the entire screen. This has the effect of clipping some of the active video from the display.

SMPTE has issued a recommended practice (RP 218) that defines 80 percent of a display, as the safe title area. This is the region of the picture that graphics or other elements can be positioned so that it is guaranteed that they will be displayed on a receiver. Safe action uses 90 percent and provides a guideline for framing the composition of subject matter in the picture. Figure 5.11 illustrates the safe action and title areas for both aspect ratios.

RP 218-2002, "Specifications for Safe Action and Safe Title Areas for Television Systems" describes a method for locating the safe action and safe title areas for television systems. Unfortunately, the recommended practice does not offer guidance in

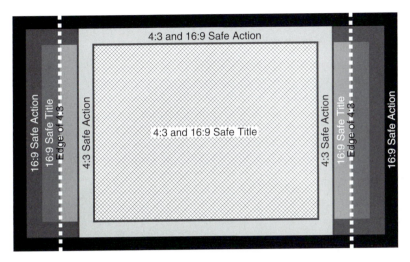

FIGURE 5.11 *Safe Title and Safe Action Areas*

situations where material generated in one aspect ratio may need to be displayed in a different aspect ratio.

Active Format Description

A new draft standard (SMPTE 2016) is expected to provide significant guidance on the proper insertion of Active Format Description codes and the size of blank bars to the left/right or the top/bottom of active video into the VANC. The method to transmit this data has been standardized in ATSC A/53, and the recommendation for receiver processing of the data in a display is published in CEA-CEB-16.

The Audio Engineering Society

Audio is an integral component of the DTV immersive experience. In the audio realm, the Audio Engineering Society (AES) develops standards related to the capture and reproduction of sounds.

The Audio Engineering Society was established in 1948. It is a professional society devoted exclusively to audio technology. Its membership of engineers, scientists and other audio authorities continues to grow throughout the world. AES sections are located in 47 geographic areas, including Australia, Canada, Europe, Japan, Mexico, South America, and the U.S.

Technical audio standards are developed by the AES and many of them have since gained acceptance by international standards organizations and have been used as the model for similar standards. AES standards are frequently included as normative references in standards developed by other organizations.

AES Standards Relevant to DTV

Two AES audio standards enable digital distribution of audio throughout a broadcast infrastructure. AES3-2003 defines a transmission format for a two-channel serial digital audio signal over a coaxial cable. It is the most common method of moving audio through the production process. The standard is also referred to as AES/EBU audio.

With the increasing use of IT equipment and pressure to maximize ROI in infrastructure, the AES has issued an audio standard that facilitates distribution over commodity network routing and switching equipment as well as coaxial cable. AES10-2003, the Multi-channel Audio Digital Interface (MADI), enables up to 64 channels of serial digital audio to be transmitted over coaxial, fiber-optic cables and IT networks.

SMPTE and Audio

AES defines the format of professional audio signals while SMPTE addresses how they are transported during production and assembly for dissemination. Generally this falls into two methods of implementation.

The first technique, distributes discrete AES audio throughout the plant as base-band signals. This requires careful timing when real-time audio is compressed and inserted into the DTV MPEG transport stream prior to processing for transmission.

The other approach to in-plant audio distribution is to insert audio into the HANC of an HD or SD SDI serial signal. The AES digital audio signals are embedded according to SMPTE 272. This method is used when uncompressed, discrete audio channels are distributed during the production and assembly process. For stereo, this requires one AES pair or two discrete channels. Similarly, for 5.1, six channels or three pairs are necessary. 20 bits of 48-KHz-sampled audio data is mapped into the ancillary data space of SMPTE 259M. SMPTE 299M applies the same methodology for embedding audio data in 292M HD serial digital video.

Additionally, a method has been developed to include uncompressed audio in an MPEG-2 transport stream as packetized AES3 48 KHz audio. The technique is useful for audio backhaul from remote broadcast locations.

Cable DTV Standards

Few would argue that cable television is a "second tier" television service anymore. For years, the majority of television viewers have been getting their TV over cable, including local and network terrestrial stations.

Society of Cable Telecommunications Engineers

The Society of Cable Telecommunications Engineers (SCTE) establishes technical standards for cable systems. The society has more than 15,000 members in over 70 countries, 3,000 of which are SCTE certified.

Founded in 1969 as the Society of Cable Television Engineers, the name was changed to reflect the variety of services delivered over the cable plant. Standards include television, connectors and high-speed data transmission over cable. SCTE is ANSI accredited, recognized by the International Telecommunication Union (ITU) and works with the European Telecommunications Standards Institute (ETSI). More than 130 MSOs, vendors and allied organizations are SCTE members.

The annual SCTE Conference on Emerging Technologies Conference focuses on the technologies expected to transform the cable telecommunications industry in the next three to five years. Attendees include chief technical officers, engineers, managers and industry analysts who come to hear a strategic view of the future from the industry's technical leaders during the comprehensive technical sessions.

Technical Committees and Standards Development

Among the many areas that SCTE technical committees are active is the implementation of DTV capabilities required by the FCC. Both of these items involve coordination of standards with other organizations.

The Emergency Alert Systems (EAS) Subcommittee works with the FCC, NCTA, FEMA and other interest groups to implement workable solutions to improve the cable TV industry's involvement in the EAS program. Members of the EAS working group are providing input to the Digital Video Subcommittee's project to revise SCTE 18 2002, "Emergency Alert Message for Cable" (a joint standard adopted by both SCTE and Consumer Electronics Association as ANSI-JSTD-042-2002).

SCTE DTV Standards

Anyone inside or outside the SCTE standards program who wishes to submit an idea for a new project can have it considered by submitting their idea on a Project Authorization Request (PAR) form to the standards staff. Every submission will be considered by the Engineering Committee and, if accepted, assigned to an appropriate subcommittee for development.

The modular system design of the ATSC standard facilitated the relatively seamless application of DTV modulation technology used by cable systems. Quadrature Amplitude Modulation (QAM) has replaced the ATSC 8-VSB transmission methodology and data protection encoding with processes deemed better suited for cable systems. The presentation, compression and transport layers utilize the ATSC specification with a few extensions.

The original cable DTV transmission standard was established in 1996 and has been updated and renamed ANSI/SCTE 07 2000, "Digital Video Transmission Standard for Television." It defines the technical methodology for DTV over cable systems. Besides the use of QAM rather than VSB modulation, there is a difference in the sequencing and parameters of noise mitigation and data protection coding step.

Additional cable DTV standards include:

- ANSI/SCTE 54 2004, "Digital Video Service Multiplex and Transport System for Cable Television," specifies how system information, program guide and scrambling will be delivered. Implementation details for emergency alerts are also described.

- ANSI/SCTE 43 2005, "Digital Video Systems Characteristics Standard for Cable Television," specifies constraints and extensions to MPEG-2.

Cable systems are dependent on satellite for program backhaul and distribution to headends. Hence, the SCTE has issued appropriate standards documents for broadband and satellite content delivery.

Institute of Electronic and Electrical Engineers

The Institute of Electronic and Electrical Engineers (IEEE) was established in 1963 with the merger of the American Institute of Electrical Engineers (AIEE), formed in 1884, and the Institute of Radio Engineers (IRE), formed in 1912. It has more than 365,000 members in more than 150 countries and hosts more than 300 conferences each year. There are about 900 active IEEE standards and more than 400 currently in development.

IEEE standards are incorporated by reference into ATSC, CEA and other DTV-related standards. Firewire (IEEE 1394) is incorporated into CEA standards and has enabled high speed transfer of content from digital cameras and other devices to personal computers.

The Broadcast Technology Society has been in existence since 1983 when the IEEE Broadcast, Cable and Consumer Electronics Society was split into separate societies. Participation of broadcast engineers in the organization can be traced back to the IEEE's roots in the IRE. Many members of the BTS are also members of SMPTE.

The IEEE Standards Association (IEEE-SA)

The IEEE Standards Association (IEEE-SA) develops global industry standards in a broad-range of industries, including IT, medical, telecommunications and new and emerging technology such as nanotechnology.

For more than a century, the IEEE-SA has administered a standards development program that offers balance, openness, due process and consensus. Each year, the IEEE-SA conducts more than 200 standards ballots, a process by which proposed standards are voted upon for technical reliability and soundness.

As a membership organization, IEEE-SA benefits from the technical diversity of its 20,000 plus participants, consisting of technology leaders from corporations, organizations, universities and government agencies. Through their collective knowledge, members contribute to the integrity and value of IEEE standards.

The Consumer Electronics Association

If a broadcaster is transmitting a signal and no one is receiving it, is content being delivered? Presentation of programming to an audience is the ultimate creative and business goal of all in the media business. Are there any artists left that create just for creation's sake? There surely aren't any broadcasters who broadcast just for technology's sake!

Devices that receive, decode and present content are the last phase in the media lifecycle. The consumer electronics industry has moved on from its advocacy of HD and DTV to implementing consumer devices that enable all to enjoy the digital media experience in all its sensory glory.

The Consumer Electronics Association (CEA) completes the chain of technical standards in the creation to consumption media lifecycle. The scope of its standards encompasses consumer electronics features, performance and interoperability. There are more than 70 committees and working groups. CEA has received stand-alone accreditation from ANSI.

DTV Relevant CEA Standards Activity

The R4 Video Systems Committee is important to establishing standards that enable the consumer transition to DTV. Working Groups are investigating areas of particular importance that include:

- R4 WG13 STB Energy Consumption is revising CEA-2013, Digital STB Background Power Consumption, to address sleep state energy consumption in terrestrial and IPTV television set top boxes (STBs). This is of particular importance as more states enact "green" laws.

- R4 WG14 AFD & Bar Data developed a bulletin (CEA-CEB-16) which provides recommendations for display actions considering presence and absence of Active Format Description (AFD, ATSC A/53) and bar data in various formats of transmitted video, for the optimal display of video and for aspect ratio adjustment.

- CEA-CEB16, "Active Format Description (AFD) & Bar Data Recommended Practice," provides guidance implementation for aspect ratio signaling, Active Format Description (AFD) and bar data. Such devices may respond to this signaling by creating an optimum (or more desirable) display, by passing this signaling through to an analog or digital output, or in preparation of a digital recording.

- CEA-CEB16 data services, such as the implementation of closed captioning, takes on an added complexity in digital, multi-channel broadcasting. The R4.3 Television Data Systems Subcommittee establishes standards and guidelines for the delivery of closed captions via television signals to the home. The work to coordinate closed captioning in receiving devices with other standards bodies ensures that DTV manufactures maintain compliance with the FCC captioning regulations.

- R4.3 WG1, "DTV Closed Captioning," is responsible for CEA 708 and is developing DTV closed captioning test bitstreams beyond v1.1 (1080i format), wherein additional formats/features will be addressed. Draft CEA-708-C, DTV Closed Captioning, incorporates the previously issued bulletins that contained additional implementation guidance.

- PSIP CEA-CEB12-A, "PSIP Recommended Practice," provides guidance for the development and implementation of ATSC PSIP-compliant receivers, cable-ready DTV receivers, personal recorders and other consumer electronics devices.

The interface to consumer devices has been an area of considerable concern to content creators and providers. With perfect digital content delivered to consumers, and with the ability to make perfect copies, protection of copyright holder's rights has been an issue.

Important interface issues that are being addressed by Working Groups include:

- The R4.8 WG1 DTV 1394 Interface has developed the CEA-775-B DTV 1394 Interface Specification that defines a specification for a baseband digital interface to a DTV using the IEEE-1394 bus and enables interoperability between a DTV and consumer digital audio/video sources including digital STBs and DVRs.

- R7 Home Network Committee provides coordination for, and encourages cooperation among, all CEA home network standardization efforts and develops and maintains all CEA standards pertaining to home networks that currently exist, are being developed or may be initiated in the future. ANSI/CEA-851-A Versatile Home Network (VHN) has been issued to ISO/IEC JTC 1/SC as a new project to become an international standard.

- CEA-851-A Versatile Home Network defines a flexible and open network architecture and communications protocol specification for digital devices in the home.

- CEA-2008 Digital Entertainment Network Initiative (DENi) specifies how more than 60 different standards interrelate and work together. Ethernet and Internet Protocol (IP) are the common network connections.

Other Societies and Organizations

In addition to standards organizations, a number of other groups are active in the broadcast industry. Some of these groups serve as advisors to the FCC on technical and regulatory issues. Others are advocacy groups that establish specifications and laboratory environments for developing technology solutions to business visions.

Many members of standards organizations belong to these groups as well. Hence their activities in multiple arenas can influence the adoption and implementation of technical standards based on a variety of different motivating factors.

The Society of Broadcast Engineers

The Society of Broadcast Engineers (SBE) was established as a non-profit organization in 1964. Membership includes broadcast professionals who are active in day-to-day broadcast operations. These include studio operators, maintenance engineers, chief engineers and engineering management.

Among its many activities, the SBE focuses on:

- communication: promotion and advancement of the profession for both theoretical and practical applications

- education: establishment of professional education, training and certifications

- professional conduct: encouraging the highest professional and ethical standards

A very important role of the SBE is its stated purpose of the "creation of working alliances and meeting of minds with all elements of the broadcast and communication industry, including the FCC." To this end, SBE regularly files comments with the FCC, reflecting the Society's views.

Two current primary goals for SBE FCC filings are protection of Broadcast Auxiliary Service (BAS) spectrum and the Emergency Alert System (EAS). Other issues may trigger national-level SBE filings. FCC filings are also sometimes triggered by member queries.

The Association for Maximum Service Television

The Association for Maximum Service Television, Inc., (MSTV) formed in 1956, has endeavored to enable reception of the highest quality, interference-free, over-the-air local television signals. MSTV participates in field-testing improvements to the digital broadcast transmission system and works closely with the ATSC. To this end, MSTV serves as a liaison between the broadcast industry and the consumer electronics, professional video and other technology industries.

For the next several years, MSTV's stated primary mission will be to insure that the transition from analog to digital transmission occurs in an economically sound and timely manner.

Important areas of MSTV activity include:

- representing the television broadcast industry on technical issues before the FCC, Congress and the Executive Branch

- promoting the deployment of HDTV as well as other advanced digital services over local broadcast television stations

- coordinating with consumer electronics and other industries to insure that production, transmission and receiving technologies are of the highest possible quality

- coordinating with other transmission systems, such as cable and satellite, to insure broadcast signals are transmitted properly and without degradation

- serving as an information resource to help television stations adopt and employ advanced technology

- working with government agencies to ensure the readiness and survivability of over-the-air television broadcasting in the event of a natural or man-made disaster

Cable Television Laboratories

Cable Television Laboratories, Inc. (CableLabs) is a non-profit research and development consortium founded in 1988 by members of the cable television industry. Its purpose is to pursue new cable telecommunications technologies and to help cable operator members integrate those technical advancements.

Areas of activity include:

- enabling interoperability among different cable systems

- facilitating retail availability of cable modems and advanced services

- helping cable operators deploy broadband technologies

- authoring specifications

- certifying products

CableLabs is funded by the monthly subscription fees paid by members as well as by testing-related fees. Cable operators from around the world are eligible to become members.

Digital Living Network Alliance

DLNA is an international, cross-industry collaboration of consumer electronics, computing industry and mobile device companies. DLNA Member Companies envision an interoperable network of personal computers, consumer electronics and mobile devices in the home and for mobile applications.

The DLNA Networked Device Interoperability Guidelines are intended to provide vendors with the information needed to build interoperable networked platforms and devices for the digital home. They specify the necessary standards and technologies that enable products to be built for networked entertainment-centric usages, allowing seamless sharing of music, photos and videos. The DLNA Interoperability Guidelines were first published in June 2004.

Summary

- Standards are a way to ensure that various systems use defined communication protocols and that the data communicated has a consistent meaning.

- DTV features and capabilities are often addressed by more than one standards body in an effort to coordinate implementation details and insure reliable operation.

- With the exception of specifications adopted as FCC Rules and Regulations, standards compliance is voluntary.

- When specifying equipment for purchase, standards compliance should be included in the system specification and purchase agreement.

6 The Transition to Metadata

Imagine life without computers. Through the use of computers at work, word processing, spreadsheets and presentation authoring have become necessities that are taken for granted. At home, an Internet connection, on-line transactions, and the ability to search and surf are part of everyday life. At school, computers are an important tool in making learning fun. Scientists have moved from slide rules to mathematical applications that rapidly solve sophisticated problems and use off-the-shelf PCs.

Computers have found their way into the broadcast infrastructure. Originally used primarily for back-office functions, then as platforms for graphic production, computers, either as embedded operating systems or application platforms, are now used for everything from media management to playout by on air server systems.

Communication between computers and applications is facilitated by metadata exchange. Even something as seemingly simple as the transfer of a file across a network requires information about the file structure in addition to the file's content to successfully complete the transaction.

Metadata has been described, ad nauseam, as "bits about the bits." It's a nice sound bite, but it's an insufficient definition in a broadcast environment. With the transition to digital technologies, nearly all aspects of broadcasting are dependent on many kinds of information that can be considered metadata.

When a search engine is used to locate an item on the Internet, a match between the search terms entered with keywords that are attached to content enables the search engine to find related Web content. These keywords are perhaps the most familiar type of "metadata" used in our online lives.

Metadata as used by broadcast systems can be categorized as two general types:

- Content-descriptive metadata is information that facilitates access to "essence", much like a label on a tape. (Essence refers to raw audio and/or video.)

- Control metadata is used for inter-process communication and enables automation of many broadcast workflows.

The Origins of Metadata in Broadcasting

Metadata has been used by broadcast systems long before the transition to digital began. When a need existed to send additional command, control and test signals with a program, ingenious communication methods were invented by engineers.

Analog Metadata

Analog NTSC uses the Vertical Blanking Interval (VBI) to communicate additional information beyond just the video and audio signals.

Closed captions are transmitted on line NTSC analog 21 using the CEA 608 standard protocol. Including this "metadata" is mandatory (for the programming covered—which is now almost all new programming). Failure to do so may be an FCC violation.

Emergency Alert System (EAS) communications are sent during the VBI. Today this includes weather warnings, all-hazard alerts and AMBER Alerts. Carriage of EAS is an FCC requirement.

Vertical Interval Test Signals (VITS) have been used to for technical purposes. The "Ghost Buster," Echo Cancellation ATSC standard A/49, "Ghost Canceling Reference Signal for NTSC," uses the VBI to send a training signal that is used by an analog receiver with the proper equipment to remove annoying ghosts.

In European PAL systems, teletext has been a part of the daily use of television for years. This information is carried in the analog VBI.

Cue tones that signal downstream broadcasters to insert local commercials can be considered control metadata. This metadata is transmitted in addition to the program content over network distribution channels.

Metadata and SDI

SDI (Serial Digital Interface) signals can carry metadata in digital form during both the vertical and horizontal blanking intervals. In digital jargon, this "metadata" is known as ancillary data, VANC for vertical and HANC and for horizontal. As in analog NTSC, closed captions, EAS and VITS can be carried in the ANC spaces as well as audio.

The "New" Metadata

In broadcasting, metadata can now be considered any information other than audio, video or data that describes content or facilitates process control in all phases of the broadcast chain: creation, assembly, distribution and consumption. This broad definition of metadata now includes not only control and content-descriptive data but also header information in IP packets, a Volume Table of Contents (VTOC) on a disk drive, information used to populate an electronic program guide and more.

Content-descriptive metadata is predominately used in media asset management (MAM) systems to classify content. Standardization efforts are being pursued by SMPTE and other organizations. MPEG working groups are addressing the need for a unified content classification system.

ASTC, SMPTE and SCTE are addressing standardization of methods of implementing control metadata used in inter-process communication. This control metadata is used to automate back-office, program assembly, digital program insertion and other functionalities by defining a common communication protocol between processes.

Communication

Communication between computers is precise. Differences in communication protocol, physical connections and operating systems can require layers of software to translate protocols as well as hardware to translate physical interfaces.

Some broadcasters still use the RS-422 interface, a communications protocol developed for the very noisy electrical and magnetic environment of an automobile assembly line. Reliable enough for mission critical, air-chain broadcast operations, VTRs and other equipment have been controlled via this interface for many years.

With the advent of computer control applications and with many of the latest generations of broadcast equipment built on PC operating systems, communication over a networked infrastructure offers a flexible method of coordinating multiple applications. The problem is that not every application speaks the same language.

That is, even if devices are interconnected over an IP network, there is no guarantee that they will communicate using a common protocol (language).

The World Wide Web has intensified the need for a common means of communication between very different computers and devices. Every computer comes with a "Web browser" of some kind that is used for many things beyond accessing the Internet. As a result, languages such as HTTP, XML, SOAP and Web Services have been developed that are universally compatible with very diverse system resources.

Modern digital broadcast systems need a defined and reliable way to communicate between resources. Standards bodies such as the ATSC and SMPTE are developing methods using XML and Web Services that can be implemented in broadcast equipment and systems to communicate with each other in a networked infrastructure. XML files are self-documenting, machine readable and can communicate technical, descriptive, administration and rights information between applications and equipment.

Content-Related Metadata

The transition to digital broadcasting includes a major change in the way content is stored and distributed. Tape has been the mainstay of acquisition and production. This is changing as content now is stored in files on servers and production moves to non-linear workflows.

With tape-based production, only one editor can work on a piece at a time. To find a particular clip (piece of content), the tape must be searched sequentially. "Sneaker net"—physical transfers of the master tape from editor to editor—moves the piece through the analog production workflow. In short, it is a linear, time-consuming process.

During the production process, content is accessible as files over a media network from centralized storage. With careful planning, production can proceed in a parallel, non-linear, time-efficient workflow. With content stored in a Storage Area Network (SAN), clips can be accessed randomly. In this way, file-based production workflows allow more than one person to access the same piece of content simultaneously.

In order to edit or assemble program elements for broadcast, you have to be able to find them. In a tapeless environment, there are no labels as the spines of tapes. Clips and graphic elements reside on disk. A simple hierarchical directory structure may suffice in the short term, but how do you find a clip or graphics element from last year and how long does it take to locate exactly what you want?

Long-term disk storage is expensive and will require the addition of more and more capacity over time. Moving content off disks to a digital tape archive is a prudent, cost-effective business practice. But you can't manually search through a robotic tape archive by loading each tape and checking the directory of folders. It is too time-consuming.

It gets worse. Let's suppose you want every presidential speech in the last decade that mentioned unemployment. How do you find these clips when they are scattered over numerous archived tapes? Even if the content is on disks, this is still a virtually impossible task by searching for files in a folder hierarchy.

Now let's add the constraint that these speeches cannot be State of the Union speeches and must have been delivered at luncheons. Finding the right clips will be like searching for many needles in a number of haystacks. Large quantities of data must be cataloged and indexed; this is where content-descriptive metadata comes in to play.

On your MARC

The media industry is not the first to be confronted with this "cataloging" dilemma. In the pre-PC age, libraries kept track of books using the Dewey decimal system and an extensive card catalog with title, author, subject and date of publication, among other information. In the 1960s, the Library of Congress initiated the Machine Readable Catalog project. Under the direction of Herriette Avram, the MARC Project computerized the entire LoC book catalog.

But the project did not stop there. It grew to an international effort and became an ISO standard. Libraries all around the world were networked and users were now able to browse the catalogs of any member library. Until the advent of the Internet, this was the largest public freely distributed information database in existence. And the amazing thing is that the MARC system has been modified and is still in use today!

Broadly speaking, an asset's metadata consists of at least three distinct types of information: descriptions of the essence, technical parameters and rights information.

- Descriptive: similar to information (title, writer, etc.) on tape labels, but for use with files

- Technical: types of audio, video, graphics, etc., and their timeline relationship

- Rights: content ownership and usage information

Metadata provides the content descriptors used in MAM systems and enables indexed content search, storage and retrieval. Assertion of rights for each new distribution platform is a source of revenue, DRM metadata can be used to track rights anywhere content may be repurposed.

When a metadata item is unknown to an application or not used by it, it is called "dark." This capability of ignoring irrelevant metadata is easily implemented by using XML.

Media Asset Management, Metadata and Workflow

The EBU/SMPTE Task Force for Harmonized Standards for the exchange of Program Material as Bitstreams addressed the requirements and technical implementation of the emerging all-digital production environment. Their reports introduced concepts that are now central to production in a file-based workflow.

A fundamental result of that effort was the definition of the term "content" as it exists in a file-based broadcast environment. The video, audio, graphics, and still images included in a file are called the "essence" while the descriptive information about the essence is called the "metadata." When rights information is associated with content is it considered an "asset." The relationships can be expressed as:

$$\text{Content} = \text{Essence} + \text{Metadata}$$
$$\text{Asset} = \text{Content} + \text{Rights Information}$$

Essence and metadata are gathered together by a "wrapper." Figure 6.1 shows how a wrapper envelopes and establishes a binding relationship of metadata to essence.

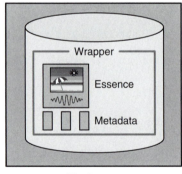

File Storage

FIGURE 6.1 *The essence and metadata, are wrapped to form a content file* (From EBU/SMPTE Task Force First Report, Courtesy SMPTE)

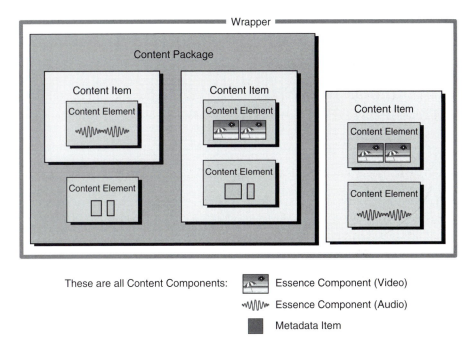

FIGURE 6.2 *Content structures that can be created from essence and metadata components* (From EBU/SMPTE Task Force First Report, Courtesy SMPTE)

Essence and metadata are considered "Content Components." Logical structures can be built from content components, as shown in Figure 6.2. They are:

- Content Element (CE): a single type of essence and related metadata

- Content Item (CI): a collection of content elements plus associative metadata

- Content Package (CP): a collection of content elements and items plus associative metadata

Metadata and the Content Lifecycle

Metadata's role in the production and distribution of programming is conceptually illustrated in Figure 6.3. The corresponding four phases in the lifecycle of metadata are (essence) creation, (program) assembly, (asset) distribution and (consumer) consumption/(library) archiving. The illustration includes representative examples of metadata attributes for each phase and associated open-standard metadata formats.

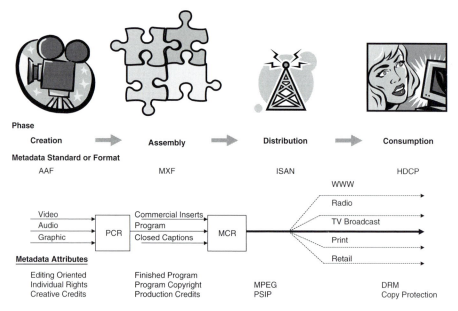

FIGURE 6.3 *The four phase content and metadata lifecycle*

A different implementation of metadata is best suited to each of the four phases. Some of methods are open standards, freely available and compatible with each other. Others are proprietary, used by groups of OEMs in a strategic alliance, and offer turnkey solutions to media asset management.

Creation

During creation of graphic elements or the ingesting of program feeds, generation of metadata will enable maintaining an audit trail during content editing. Appropriate descriptive information such as time, date, location, talent, director, producer, etc., should be logged and associated with the newly created essence. Technical details pertinent to format conversion, color correction, equipment calibration, compression encoding, Edit Decision Lists (EDL), transitions and steps taken in the editing process are all metadata that is essential to record for future editing and program assembly. Rights must be associated with each element so individual contributors can receive production credits and royalty payments.

Assembly

In the assembly phase, all content elements (video, audio and graphics) are assembled into a program, laid off to tape or stored on a server. The program is now ready for distribution. From this point on, there is little need for much of the metadata pertinent to editing the original source material, because a clip's production process has little to do with its integration into a program. Technical information necessary for consumer equipment decoding resides in the digital program stream. The creator's contributions and copyright information have been cataloged and are traceable by reference in this stage, and digital rights management (DRM) capabilities should be activated before publication and loss of control.

Distribution

In a Master Control Room (MCR), the program, commercials, logos and other elements go to air as scheduled on the playlist/rundown. Each of the three primary types of content-related metadata (descriptive, technical and rights), is now contained in the program stream. Technical information is conveyed in the MPEG video or AC-3 audio packets. Program descriptions are communicated by PSIP. Conditional access systems such as CableCard may limit consumption of an asset and redistribution rights management may be accomplished via a "Broadcast Flag" or proprietary DRM techniques.

Consumption

The consumer in the emerging networked home media environment demands instant access and retrieval of any desired media item for presentation on any device. "Recommender Systems" that sift through the available metadata to find just the kind of "asset" you might find interesting and alert you to its availability are a necessity to maximize your ability to locate new programs amidst the abundance of content available. Creator's rights must be enforced with metadata now that the content is out of the originator's control.

For Future Generations

The National Digital Information Infrastructure and Preservation Program (NDIIPP) is an effort by the Library of Congress to build a national infrastructure for the collection and long-term preservation of digital content. Appropriate metadata, attached at various times during asset creation and distribution, should be compatible with this public archiving effort. Television broadcasts are historical events in and of themselves. This expansion of today's libraries to media libraries should be supported by the media industry.

Workflow Enhancements

The benefits to be realized in workflow efficiency and improvements in a digital infrastructure from the intelligent use of metadata include:

- Streamlined asset retrieval. Intelligent assignment and use of metadata facilitates efficient searches and saves time retrieving when compared to locating content stored on tape or other physical media.

- Re-editing is facilitated because the original edit decisions are stored in metadata and source material is easily traced and retrieved.

- Content rights clearance and payment can be simplified by DRM metadata. When the process can be automated, clearance for use of content can be streamlined and an asset's value maximized.

- Integration with back-office functions and event scheduling eliminates tedious, repetitive manual logging of content, avoids clerical errors, and assists in automated billing and royalty payments.

Issues

As useful as metadata is in a digital broadcast environment, it does come with cautions. Among these is the process of creating the metadata, the resultant file structure and, as always, creator's rights.

Element Creation

Where, when and how metadata is captured can become a significant task. Imagine attaching metadata to programs on thousand of tapes in a library archive. Obviously, there is a need to automate metadata generation for a task like this. Therefore, it is important to incorporate metadata with new essence from the initial moment of acquisition or creation rather than add it at a later time.

A careful analysis of workflow and how metadata is transferred across all processes in an organization will help head off asset management problems before they happen. It is extremely important to understand how metadata is used, propagated and persists through the various processes involved in content creation and distribution. This will enable intelligent assignment of relevant information that can be used during the lifetime of the asset.

Flattening

As elements are created and assembled and the finished program is distributed through a transmission channel, it is desirable to include some, but not all, of the metadata pertinent to each phase. This reduction of the metadata is known as "flattening." For example, the editing information used during program production is of no use to a viewer and can be discarded.

Flattening files is important because transmission channels have limited data capacity. For example if a content file (essence and metadata) totals 100 MB for a 30-second clip, the associated data rate would be 800 Mb/30 sec or 26.67 Mbps. If metadata is 25 percent of the file, then flattening the file by removing the unneeded editing information reduces the data rate to 20 Mbps.

Rights and Responsibilities

Rights management of program elements during program creation and rights management of a completed program after dissemination to the consumer are two separate issues. Prior to distribution, securing copyright clearance is the responsibility of the program originator.

When this content is assembled for consumption, tracking the rights of creative contributors is the responsibility of the broadcaster. However, legal responsibility for enforcement of these rights after the content is disseminated is unclear.

Copy protection technologies in the consumer environment, such as High-bandwidth Data Copy Protection (HDCP), are intended to stop unauthorized copying and distribution of programming once it reaches the consumer. Copyright and DRM metadata needs to be persistent through all phases of creation assembly, distribution and consumption.

Interoperability

There are conflicting approaches to metadata implementation: open standards versus proprietary systems. Open standards (or open source) solutions are license- and royalty-free and often developed by ad-hoc contributions of code developers. Implementation and support is left to the user. Proprietary systems are developed by a company or organization that holds intellectual property rights and charges a license fee for using the technology. For this fee, implementation and maintenance support is provided.

This results in an inherent lack of interoperability among proprietary file formats and can cause difficulties when trying to create content with one vendor's application and then edit it with a different vendor's application.

To make matters worse, even when the same metadata "standard" is implemented by different vendors, problems with file compatibility still can occur. Not all implementations of a standard are equally compliant.

Compatibility and interoperability of various metadata implementations is now becoming a reality. Open source efforts such as the Advanced Authoring Format (AAF) and the Material eXchange Format (MXF) in particular are gaining widespread broadcast industry acceptance.

Unique Identification

With the increasing dependency on metadata for content management, a means must exist to unambiguously identify content. SMPTE has established a methodology that guarantees generation of a unique file identifier.

A Unique Material Identifier (UMID), defined in SMPTE 330, is a method of unambiguously identifying content and can be used to link content through its lifecycle. UMIDs consist of a SMPTE 298M Universal Label and a Material Number. An additional "Source Pack" extension includes time/date and location information. Recommended use of UMIDs is described in RP 205.

SMPTE 298M, "Universal Labels for Unique Identification of Digital Data," defines the syntax of universal labels and a labeling mechanism that can be used to identify the type and encoding of data. It is intended to function across all types of digital communications protocols and message structures. UMIDs are attached to the data they identify. The label and data travel together through communications channels. This enables tracing labels (and content) through its distribution path.

Use of a UMID is only one of the items necessary to enable transparent file transfers between applications and implementation of automated production processes. To attain this goal, definitions of the structure of content files must be established.

Specifications are being implemented so that appropriate metadata file formats for interoperability between each stage of the broadcast chain become an operational reality. Standards bodies are working to define a common set of metadata type definitions needed in workflow scenarios for each use of content during its lifecycle. Most importantly, the solution enables tracking of content and elements through the production, transmission and consumption lifecycle.

The Advanced Authoring Format (AAF)

The Advanced Authoring Format (AAF) is designed for use during file-based production and editing. Developed by a media industry coalition, the AAF Association (www.AAFAssociation.org) builds on the work of the SMPTE/EBU Task Force.

It has developed a software standard for implementation of metadata and registry (dictionary) of metadata terms. The metadata registry includes technical, descriptive and rights information.

AAF uses the SMPTE metadata dictionary defined in RP-210. The dictionary contains descriptive elements, some of which are associated as "sets" that have been grouped together for a particular use. These collections of items are known as Interchange Objects.

The AAF data model defines how content is comprised of components, represented as classes of Interchange Objects. Complex Content Packages are constructed of data structures built from Interchange Objects, as shown in Figure 6.4.

Central to locating and using content is the need for a unique identifier. AAF uses an AUID (Authoring Unique ID) that is mapped to SMPTE labels. Therefore,

Wrapper

Content Package

Content Item

Content Item

Content Item

Content Element

Content Element

Content Element

Content Element

Content Element

Content Element

Content Element

Content Element

Content Element

Content Package

Content Element

These are all Content Components:

 Essence Component (Video)   Metadata Item

〜∿∿∿∿〜 Essence Component (Audio)   ▯ Vital Metadata (e.g. Essence Type)

■ Essence Component (Other Data)   ▮ Association Metadata (e.g. Timecode)

FIGURE 6.4 *AAF Files Contain Complex Content Packages Built of Interchange Objects* (From Understanding AAF, Courtesy AAF Association)

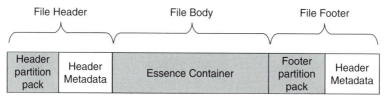

FIGURE 6.5   *A Simple MXF File Structure* (From EG-41, Courtesy SMPTE)

any metadata implementation that includes a UMID can link to AAF files. AAF files can also reference and incorporate other AAF files. In this way a record of the creative history of the piece or clip is maintained.

Perhaps the most important aspect of AAF is the relationship it shares with the MXF specification used for managing a finished program.

Material Exchange Format (MXF)

The Material Exchange Format (MXF) is a subset of AAF and intended to be used for distribution and archiving. It is not designed to be used for content management during the editing process.

Essence and metadata are "wrapped" with MXF header data to produce an MXF file. The structure of an MXF file is independent of the format of the essence. MXF files are self-contained and do not reference other external MXF files.

MXF file structure commonality allows transfer of a file to any MXF-capable device. Yet to open and used the content, an appropriate decoder must be accessible.

Figure 6.5 presents a simple MXF file. The File Body consists of an Essence Container while File Headers and Footers have a Header Partition Pack and Header Metadata. These partitions are optional and implemented depended upon application features.

An optional but recommended Index Table facilitates conversion from time code to byte offsets in the container. This technique can be used to enable partial file restores.

Two SMPTE Engineering Guidelines are available to aid in implementing MXF based systems.

- EG 41-2004, the "Material Exchange Format (MXF) Engineering Guideline," describes the technology, the names of the various elements and provide examples of ways in which MXF may be used in the real world applications.

- EG 42-2004, "Material Exchange Format (MXF)—MXF Descriptive Metadata," is intended to provide guidance for the use of MXF descriptive metadata schemes and explains the common structural metadata components by which all MXF descriptive metadata schemes can be related to the essence they describe.

Metadata Registries

Standardization of metadata terminology is the means to interoperability among systems that use content, such as MAMs, editing applications and home digital networks.

Consistent properties, attributes and naming conventions need to be established. Yet different manufacturers and organizations use different terms or the same terms in different ways. For example, is it a "home run," "homer" or an "HR"? The MAM search engine will need to know that each of these terms has the same meaning. Consistent use of case may be necessary—a "Home Run" may not be a "home run" across all platforms. Potentially illegal characters such as "/" or "@" may cause problems.

If these conventions are not enforced across the enterprise, assets will be "unsearchable" and virtually lost. A solution is to use standardized terms that are referenced to a metadata dictionary.

There are a number of metadata registries in existence that facilitate dictionary reference to metadata terminology. The purpose of a metadata registry is to identify the meaning of a term by an application when a particular code point (a unique sequence of bytes that identifies an individual item) is parsed. To do this, the application must know which metadata registry has been used to associate metadata with essence.

The SMPTE Registration Authority (www.smpte-ra.org) provides a public repository for several labeling standards. This structure is not a normative reference, but it provides sufficient information in a compact form to enable users to locate metadata items and to provide an easy tool by which new metadata items can be placed within the metadata dictionary.

The metadata dictionary is a complete list of metadata elements identified by the last eight octets (bytes) of the SMPTE universal label (UL). The UL (which is included in a UMID) defines a tree structure with a multiplicity of branches (called nodes) and the metadata items are defined as leaves. The dictionary specifies which ULs are nodes and which are leaves.

For libraries and long term preservation of digital assets, the Open Archival Information System (OAIS) is developing a reference model to enable exchange of metadata among registries.

International Standard Audiovisual Number

Even though use of MXF has reduced the amount of editing-related metadata associated with content used to create a program, it is still more information than is necessary during distribution. ISO 1570, "Information and documentation—The International Standard Audiovisual Number" (ISAN), contains just enough information to uniquely identify each program that is broadcast.

For ISAN purposes, an audio-visual work is defined as a "work consisting of a sequence of related images, with or without accompanying sound, which is intended to be made visible as a moving image through the use of devices, regardless of the medium of initial or subsequent fixation." An ISAN consists of 16 hexadecimal digits followed by an alphanumeric check character. An additional eight hex digits are an optional version extension.

Commercials, feature films, live events, sporting events and music videos are among the types of content eligible for ISAN registration. Audio recordings, soundtracks, storyboards, out-takes, still photographs and other similar works are not assigned ISAN numbers.

ISAN follows a registry model. The centralized database is maintained by the ISAN International Agency (ISAN-IA), located in Geneva, Switzerland. The ISAN registration database includes additional descriptive information that is associated with the ISAN. This metadata set consists of items such as title, year of first publication, directors, cast, type, script writers and additional information.

A regional registration agency accepts applications for ISAN Registrant status and can be made by a producer or a producer's authorized proxy. The applicant must certify that all descriptive information provided is accurate. In the U.S., Microsoft Studios and Secure Path are ISAN RAs.

An ISAN is obtained by a registrant by logging on to the ISAN System and entering the required descriptive information. This data is added to the ISAN System Central Repository and creates a permanent identifier for the work.

Public readers can access the ISAN database (www.isan.org) and query by ISAN number or title. Registered readers pay a fee and can make mass queries and generic queries based on descriptive information.

ISAN is implemented by the ATSC as specified in A/57 and identifies program, episode and version of content delivered in MPEG transport streams. An ISAN can be carried in MPEG-2 transport streams, SMPTE 292 VANC and ATSC PSIP information. Program material that contains an ISAN can be traced back thought the content lifecycle.

Consumption and Metadata

Ultimately, the program arrives at the consumer. At this point, the media stream structure is parsed and interpreted. The "asset" provides rights information facilitating or limiting access to content. "Content" is broken down into metadata that describes the essence and can enable EPG, iTV and recommender features. The essence is extracted and presented.

In the consumer environment, various metadata schemes are proliferating. Compatibility between systems is an issue. Of paramount concern at this point in the content lifecycle is the application of rights management.

High-bandwidth Digital Content Protection (HDCP) is intended for networked consumer devices and takes a large step towards solving consumer device copy protection interoperability problems. Both the Digital Video Interface (DVI) and High-bandwidth Digital Multimedia Interface (HDMI) specifications use HDCP.

There are three parts to an HDCP implementation: authentication, encrypted content transfer and renewability. Authentication is accomplished between a sending and receiving device by verifying that the receiving device demonstrates knowledge of secret keys.

Next, content is encrypted by a logical combination of bits with a pseudo-random data stream produced by the HDCP cipher. A cipher is the method used to encrypt content. Pseudo-random describes a technique that generates a series of apparently random bits (1s and 0s) using a mathematical relationship that can be repeated exactly.

Renewability, the third part of the HDCP method, is intended to eliminate any risk that the security of the content transfer has been compromised. Through a process defined in the license agreement, the Digital Content Protection LLC (the HDCP technology licensing administrator) may determine that the system has been compromised. It then places the key on a revocation list. System Renewability Messages (SRMs) are delivered with the content. The transmitter must check SRMs when they are delivered and then store the revocation list. Content will not be sent to receivers with authorization keys on the revocation list.

Digital Rights Management

Administration of rights is a source of revenue for broadcasters and creative artists. Any new digital distribution channel has associated content rights. Distribution licenses are granted for monetary consideration. Artists are paid performance royalties.

Every item in a broadcast must have persistent and interoperable DRM metadata through the creation/assembly/distribution/consumption chain. This is becoming increasingly more difficult as content is consumed on a wider variety of platforms. Automated tracking of creator's rights has yet to be facilitated through the complete content lifecycle, across all delivery channels and for every presentation device.

What Are Copyrights?

Many people in broadcasting and the media business talk about DRM, but few seem to know exactly what copyrights protect. Rights get cloudy when applied to new distribution channels and reproduction technologies. Often, there are few, if any, legal precedents to follow.

Consider this scenario. At a sporting event, music played over the house PA is disseminated during transmission. Who pays the royalty due for public performance of this copyrighted material?

Article I, Section 8, Clause 8 of the U.S. Constitution established the legal right of inventors and creators to financially exploit their creations. The Copyright Act of 1790 granted American authors the right to print, re-print, or publish their work for a period of 14 years and to renew for another 14. There have been major revisions to the act in 1831, 1870, 1909 and 1976.

Section 106 of the 1976 Copyright Act generally gives the owner of copyright the exclusive right to do and to authorize others to do the following:

- Reproduce (copy) the work

- Prepare derivative works

- Distribute copies of the work to the public

- Perform the work publicly

- Display the copyrighted work publicly

- Perform the sound recording publicly by means of a digital audio transmission

Fair Use?

Copying of copyrighted material was indisputably illegal in all circumstances until the "fair use" doctrine was established by a 5-4 vote of the Supreme Court in *Sony Corp v. Universal City Studios*, 1984.

Personal copying of copyrighted works is established by this "fair use" doctrine. With the introduction of the concept of time shifting and the proliferation technology that simplifies content copying, a generational slippery slope has lead to copyright anarchy. Many consider copying a right, not an "illegal" act.

Perhaps a new model is necessary in the digital era. An argument has been put forth by some that copyrights restrict innovation. Yet one can argue that copyrights stimulate originality and creativity by using market survivability to reward quality and relevance. A technology organization would rarely, if ever, advocate releasing its intellectual property without license fees. Yet that is what is being asked of creators.

CDs and DVDs are relatively cheap because of the constitutionally mandated restrictions on copying and distribution. If free copying were permitted, maybe instead of $15 a CD, the cost should be $150 or maybe $300, knowing that a royalty will never be paid for copies. But if an artist is entitled to even just a paltry 10 cents per copy sold, a million-seller would generate $100,000!

The Millennium Digital Copyright Act of 1998 has extended copyright to include new forms of digital delivery, in particular the Internet, and prohibits circumvention of copy protection technology. It also extends U.S. copyright law globally and implements two World Intellectual Property Organization (WIPO) treaties.

Another rewrite of copyright laws may be triggered by the recent efforts of Internet based companies to digitize books found in major libraries. This use of copyrighted content has generated lawsuits by the Authors Guild and the American Association of Publishers. At issue is the requirement of obtaining a creator's consent before scanning the work.

(By the way, the answer to the sports arena scenario is: the venue pays a blanket license fee to ASCAP, BMI or SESAC for playing songs over the stadium PA. The broadcaster doesn't have any obligation to pay royalties for the song's incidental inclusion in a broadcast.)

Copyright Protection Goes Digital

During the development of digital media systems and standards, the issue of copyright protection was considered. AES/EBU, SPDIF, MPEG/ATSC and AC-3 specifications defined a one-bit copyright flag that has proven to be easily circumvented and completely insufficient for practical DRM enforcement.

Controversy has surrounded the "Broadcast Flag" Redistribution Control Descriptor (RCD) specified in ATSC A/65A. Although the FCC established rules that mandated its use, the Supreme Court ruled that the mandate is beyond the scope of the FCC's legal jurisdiction. Congress is now reconsidering the issue.

Cable systems address copy issues by using conditional access technologies in VOD and PPV applications. CableCARD technology provides copy protection for HDTV-ready (tuner equipped) DTVs. In the future, Downloadable Conditional Access Systems (DCAS) will enable content protection without a CableCARD.

A Content Protection System (CPS) must be tamper resistant. The content delivery channel must be managed and protected. Content Protection System Architectures (CPSA) integrate technologies that address copy and playback control using watermark and encryption techniques.

Watermarks are low-bit-rate information embedded in content, persistent and transparent to the end user. They cannot be removed. Unencrypted content carries "watermark CMI (Content Management Information)" usage rules. Watermarks enable a forensic investigation to trace illegal copies back through the distribution chain and identify the guilty parties.

Encryption encodes content in a way that renders it useless without a means to convert it back to its original form. This is accomplished thorough use of a key that authorizes decryption of protected content. Frequently, a second key is used in the decryption algorithm.

> Even sophisticated DRM methodologies for encryption and licensing have not been powerful enough to stop content pirates. Amazingly, illegal DVD copies of movies have hit the street before the movie release date!

Broadcaster's Responsibility

Broadcasters are not in the business of illegally distributing copyrighted material but are broadcasters required to pass DRM data? If so, DRM metadata persistence becomes a legal matter. If they fail to do so, are they liable for consumer copyright infringement?

MAM systems can incorporate rights management. Is a traffic light alert: green, clear; yellow, caution; red, danger sufficient? Content goes to air, worry about the rights later. Bad idea if it may cost you $100,000 or more for a willful copyright violation! Or do you take a cautious approach and restrict MAM publication of material without rights clearance and possibly inhibit the production process?

The point of this discussion is that when content is in a file format and stored in a MAM system, content has the potential to make it to air without any person verifying rights clearance. So when implementing a DRM system, great care must be taken to identify and review any content with questionable rights clearance, before it makes it to air.

Control Metadata

With the advent of networked digital broadcast systems, an opportunity exists to standardize communication between back office, production and broadcast processes and create an automated workflow. Communication between these "islands" has usually been by manual data entry or automated to some degree by custom software applications.

The transition to digital has precipitated a need for a transition to digital workflows. In a digital workflow, processes that were previously on virtual "islands" can now communicate with each other and automate content transfer and control information exchange. In this way, consistent information to receive, schedule, track and air content and then verify that it ran, error-free and as scheduled, is communicated among processes.

The Big Picture

There are four general processes that facilitate the assembly and distribution of programs.

- Creating a rundown with commercial spots

- Generation of PSIP information

- Movement of content to servers, both program and commercial

- Inclusion of switching cues for content insertion by downstream broadcasters

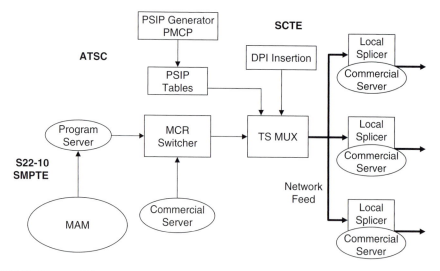

FIGURE 6.6 *PSIP, S22-10 and SCTE control metadata communication system diagram*

Figure 6.6 conceptually depicts the overall system whose communication and data transfer processes are being automated. Areas of work by ATSC, S22-10 and the SCTE are indicated.

Rundowns

Rundowns (or playlists) have been used in TV broadcasting since day one. Once hand-written or typed on a piece of paper, today rundowns are produced by software applications. These systems enable automated content movement to servers and playout to air. Electronic rundowns can easily be altered to change respond to the demands of a live broadcast.

PSIP Generation

Inclusion of PSIP (ATSC A/65) data in the transport stream is a metadata intensive process. PSIP (as discussed in Chapter 5) delivers the information necessary to assemble a program and populate an Electronic Program Guide (EPG). Automated updating, in a timely manner, of PSIP information is necessary for an EPG and for the EPG to interface with a Digital Video Recorder (DVR) in a STB.

Information for PSIP tables comes from numerous places. The MAM system contains content descriptive metadata. Program scheduling has air time data that is used to build the rundown. Other information is carried as ancillary data in SDI signals.

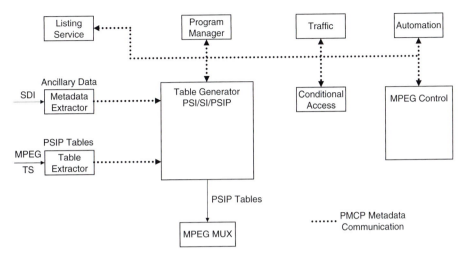

FIGURE 6.7 *PMCP Metadata System Architecture*

Methods for using ancillary data space to carry process control data in real-time in a broadcast environment is being investigated with the goal of developing industry standards. ATSC, SMPTE and SCTE are working on standardizing interoperable communications methods in this area.

The need for process automation starts with PSIP data for EPGs but moves well beyond this in scope. Figure 6.7 is a block diagram of systems that, in an ideal broadcast operations center, would transparently automate PSIP generation. Operator intervention would only be necessary to avoid an impending problem or to take corrective action once a malfunction has occurred.

Keeping Program Information Up to Date

Because many systems used in preparing PSIP tables often work independent of each other, manual processes link the information among systems, frequently with the same information being entered repeatedly. A manual workflow is time-consuming and error-prone. Automated inter process control metadata communication can streamline the process and insure consistent information across the workflow.

PSIP is required by the FCC to be carried by Terrestrial and Cable operators. To be compliant with PSIP requirements, sufficient information is necessary to populate the following PSIP tables, at the minimum:

- MGT: Master Guide Table

- VCT: Virtual Channel Table

- STT: System Time Table

- EIT: Event Information Table

- RRT: Rating Region Table

- ETT: Extended Text Table

The PSIP generation process must dynamically update these FCC-mandated data tables with information that can sometimes change very close to air time. This can pose a problem. DTV receivers may only download new PSIP information on power-up. Similarly, STBs may only download PSIP data when they are turned on or in a stand-by mode during non-viewing hours, typically overnight. Last-minute program changes may not be downloaded in a timely manner. This can cause the EPG to be out of date.

Recognizing the need for automating the PSIP generation process, an ATSC working group was established to investigate methods to coordinate metadata across PSIP generation systems. ATSC A/76, "Programming Metadata Communication Protocol Standard" (PMCP), is the result of this working group's efforts.

PMCP defines a method, based on XML, for communicating metadata used by PSIP generation systems. The A/76 document defines the PMCP XML Schema. This metadata can also be entered in the transport stream and used for backhaul or downstream implementations.

Automating Workflows with Control Metadata

It was recognized that some of the metadata used in PMCP for PSIP generation is also used by traffic and automation systems. Program management and content delivery systems also provide information that is used in generation of program schedules. Generation of as-run logs that can communicate with ad sales and billing helps streamline and remove human errors from what is now often a tedious manual process.

Work in this area naturally falls into the SMPTE's production standards domain and is addressed by the S22-10 Working Group. Its charter is to develop methods that enable the dynamic updating of program and commercial spot information throughout a facility. This information can be used to automate movement of content to playout servers, play the clip or commercial spot, and then move it off the server to an archive or remove it from the MAM.

Intra-facility movement of content can be accomplished by asset management applications. Media Object Server (MOS) enabled systems can transcode and move content based on playlist entries and "folder drops" (see side bar). This type of process automation minimizes the need for operator intervention, reduces errors and saves time.

Folder Drop

A technique that is used by many applications, as well as in both PMCP and the S22-10 protocol, is the "deposit" of a file (either when it is created or by a file copy) in a designated folder. When this file is instantiated in the folder, actions occur based on defined workflows. In one instance, an e-mail notification may be sent to an art director telling them that a lower third is ready for review. In another case, a folder drop may initiate transcoding a file from a graphics format to a broadcast video format.

Inter-Process Metadata Communication

Since commercials are the primary source of income for broadcasters, sophisticated, organization specific workflows and processes have evolved to get them to air. These are long-standing processes that the organization has confidence in and are generally reluctant to alter.

The spot has to be delivered to the broadcaster. It must be cataloged, QC'ed and assigned an identification number. It also must meet technical, time and editorial requirements.

ISCI and Ad-ID

For years, the advertising industry and many broadcasters have used an ISCI number for commercial identification. The ISCI numbering system is now in the process of being upgrading to an Ad-ID (www.ad-id.org), a 12-digit coding system under the auspices of the Association of National Advertisers (www.ana.net). The naming system to support identification of multiple channels is being developed by the AAAA/TVB Joint Task Force.

Broadcasters are rapidly moving from hand delivery to electronic transfer of commercial spots and content over high-performance wide area networks. A number of companies offer complete commercial spot and program content delivery solutions. Integrating this process with in-plant systems in an automated fashion would be advantageous and is a goal of standards activity.

With most modern facilities using some form of automated play-to-air capability, information about the content (metadata) must be entered into a traffic system and into a playlist. After it finally gets to air, an as-run list verifies that it did get to air and an air check recording vouches for the quality of the transmission.

One Vocabulary

It is in the best interest of all broadcasters and system vendors to standardize system interoperability for the entire content delivery and playout automation process. Yet many a manufacturer holds onto a proprietary philosophy. This locks broadcasters into a single vendor's solution.

There is hope. Mentioned earlier, the SMPTE S22-10 Working Group is addressing this conundrum. Sometimes referred to as the Broadcast Data Exchange (BDX), this Working Group's mission is to establish interoperability among the programming, ad sales, traffic, automation and content delivery systems, all of which play a role getting commercials and content into the facility and to air by defining control metadata communication interfaces and methodology.

The key to tracking the content through the workflow is a unique identifier. Yet there can often be a number of IDs (house number, ISCI, UMID) used to identify the same piece of content. A tiered ID structure is used where primary, secondary and local IDs can be consolidated into one ID form. A PMCP XML schema facilitates these three levels of content ID and enables broadcasters to use different IDs to reference the same content by various systems in the workflow.

Content Transfer

Two types of transport mechanisms implement the S22-10 protocol for moving information throughout the facility: file-based or connection-based.

File-based transport is used when large amounts of data transfers do not require critical timing or successful transfer acknowledgement. There is a common file naming scheme and receiver notification when the common folder drop technique is used.

Connection-based transport uses TCP/IP protocol, with a defined port number. Receiving devices act as servers while sending devices are clients. Clients initiate socket connection and data exchange. Handshake acknowledgement enables reliable transfers but at the expense of speed.

A standard language for web services messages, Simple Object Access Protocol (SOAP) communications are carried over Hypertext Transfer Protocol (HTTP) as the interface between systems. SOAP servers advertise themselves as objects in system resource registries and use an API.

System security is a major concern. After all, any successful attack to this system hits broadcasters in their pocketbooks. Implementation of the commonly used Secure Sockets Layer (SSL) or Transport Layer Security (TLS) techniques is recommended. This will help insure secure, encrypted communication. A new SMPTE ad hoc group has been formed to address and resolve security issues.

Perfect Harmony

SMPTE and ATSC working group members have made a conscious effort to ensure these two standards compliment each other. The working groups interact and are evolving concurrently. PCMP preceded S22-10. S22-10 wanted to use an XML tool with a higher degree of abstraction and module independence in related work. Since PCMP was open and being updated to V3.0 to support ACAP data broadcasting, modularization of the XML code was also included in version 3.0 and published in A/76A. PMCP V3.0 is now in the process of ATSC formal adoption. Figure 6.8 shows how the work of S22-10 complements ATSC PMCP.

This modularization of PMCP enables using XML "include" directives, similar to the technique used in C coding. In this way, PMCP modules point to schemas that can be used in S22-10 standards. Additionally, ATSC data transport methods are similar to the S-22 file -based and connection-based methods.

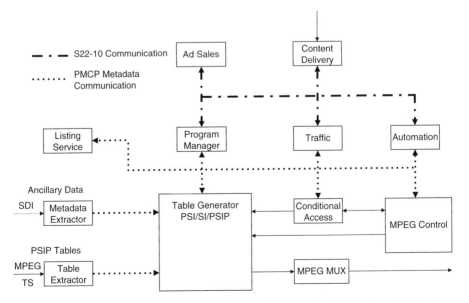

FIGURE 6.8 *PMCP and S22-10 Inter-process Communication System Architecture*

Include Directives

Rewriting code for common functions slows down the application authoring process and increases the possibility of errors. Rather than develop drag and drop, file copy and other commoditized features, inclusion of code modules that enable these basic features in a library relieves the programmer from authoring code for this task and also helps to insure error free operation. To accomplish this, libraries of functions such as Input and Output functions or Math operations are incorporated in an application by using an "Include" directive at the beginning of a program. This is why the coordination of ATSC and S22-10 code modules and sharing of code libraries is important.

Coordinating both content-descriptive and control-metadata is necessary to automate the assembly of program elements for dissemination. Metadata and the SMPTE Registration Authority simplify cataloging and retrieval of content. PMCP and the work of SMPTE S22-10 are automating PSIP generation, content delivery and playout.

Work is underway in SMPTE to develop engineering guidelines, recommended practices and standards for control metadata communication. RP 207, "Transport of Program Description Data in Vertical Ancillary Data Packets," describes how a packet can carry data which defines characteristics of the video and audio program material. It can be used by station equipment in producing PSIP data in accordance with ATSC A/65.

DPI Standards

The automated inclusion of Digital Program Insertion (DPI) signaling information is a natural extension of ATSC PMCP and SMPTE S22-10. This control metadata (in effect, digital cue-tones) facilitates the process of program and commercial insertion further downstream by affiliates and MSOs.

DPI technology is rapidly replacing audio cue tones. DPI is the inclusion of metadata that directs an MPEG-2 transport stream "splicer" to cut from one program to another. These programs may be included in a Multi-Program Transport Stream (MPTS) or in separate MPTSs or each may be in a Single Program Transport Stream (SPTS).

However, rather that switching from program to program, it is much more likely that a commercial will be inserted downstream.

Standardization of the DPI process, to date, has fallen under the auspices of SCTE. A series of standards defines the scenario and specifies the methodology to be implemented:

- SCTE 30, "Digital Program Insertion API," defines the communication protocol between servers and splicers for insertion of content in to an MPEG 2 transport stream.

- SCTE 35, "Digital Program Insertion Cuing Message for Cable," specifies methods for notifying a splicer of upcoming splice points. This information is carried in a Splice Information Table with its own PID.

- SCTE 67, "Applications Guidelines for SCTE 35 2001," describes overall system implementation.

- SCTE 118-3 2006, "Program-Specific Ad Insertion—Traffic System to Ad Insertion System File Format Specification," defines an ad insertion system as "a complete hardware and software solution that interprets the schedule file, streams content when triggered based on the schedule file, logs insertion results and returns a verification to the traffic and billing system."

Packetized compressed content in transport streams does not have a vertical blanking interval. Data is continuously delivered without a direct correlation with real-time. (The assembly instructions, Presentation Time Stamps (PTS), inform the DTV receiver as to when content is to be presented.) Transport stream splicing is simplified when it occurs on I-frame boundaries, since I-frames can be decoded without referring to nay other compressed P or B frames.

Buffer overflow (when the data coming into the buffer exceeds the rate at which it is being read out, causing the buffer to eventually fill up) or underflow (when data is read out of the buffer faster than it is coming in, meaning eventually there is no data to read out of the buffer) is an issue because there is no way to determine the size of a compressed frame. It is dependent on GOP structure and scene complexity.

Summary

- Increasing dependence on all forms of metadata is a characteristic of digital production, broadcasting and consumption.

- Content-descriptive metadata facilitates management of assets while control metadata automates operations.

- Without integrated, consistent, interoperable metadata, ubiquitous, transparent distribution and consumption of digital audio and video content may never become a reality.

- Metadata must be persistent. It is analogous to a digital label in a tapeless world. Lose the metadata and you've lost the content, therefore it must be maintained through all phases of the content lifecycle.

- The protection of rights must be maintained, but balanced with the ability to locate and preview content before a purchase transaction.

- The ATSC and SMPTE are developing methods for automating PSIP generation and the communication of other control information among production processes.

- Digital Program Insertion technology is rapidly replacing audio cue tones.

7 Emerging Technologies and Standards

There are two things that are indisputable about the transition to digital broadcasting: change is the only constant and broadcast systems will continue to increase in complexity. As one moderator put it at a 2005 IBC session addressing the education of modern broadcast engineers, in 20 years they will look back and long for the days when systems were "simple"!

The media business is at a point of disruption; technology is advancing in complexity at an ever-increasing rate. It is important for a technology-dependent organization to stay ahead of this wave. Therefore, it is in a broadcaster's best interest to keep an eye on emerging technologies and industry standards.

Application or enabling technology?

Many are in search of "killer apps." HDTV and interactive TV are among things that have been heralded as killer applications. But HDTV and iTV are not killer apps. They are enabling technologies. The content delivered over HDTV, such as a stunning visual with immersive surround sound, is the killer application of HDTV technology. Similarly, iTV, in and of itself, is not a killer app. It will enable the development of applications that may become fads and financial successes. So by definition, an enabling technology is the platform for killer apps, not the killer app in and of itself.

Topics discussed in this chapter are on the cusp of deployment, including advances in presentation, compression, delivery and distribution, targeted DTV advertising, and a multiplatform emergency alert system. These are technologies that are impacting the media business now as well as over the next few years. As rapidly as technology is developed and can impact the direction of the industry, it would be impossible to speculate more than a few years into the future.

Technology and Standards Development

To prepare for the immediate future, maintaining an awareness of relevant technological research and advanced systems development is a necessity, especially in a large media organization. Each broadcaster has unique infrastructure requirements for their creative workflows and business models. Yet their engineering departments often are used for support and caught in a fire-fighting mentality, barely keeping on the air, let alone researching what the next major technology step for the organization should be.

An advanced technology development lab provides an environment where new equipment and systems can be tested and evaluated. This helps ensure that technology investments will be maximized and that systems will operate in a robust, resilient and predictable manner when installed and commissioned.

A proactive development lab can facilitate the design and integration of complex systems, portions of which are designed and maintained by various technical departments. It is a place where all stakeholders can work on the complete system as a team.

The lab is also a place to collaborate with vendors and influence the development of new features in equipment that will meet future technology requirements. Collaborative relationships can be built with vendors that can lead to confidence in their company and the engineering and manufacture of their equipment.

"Type Acceptance" of equipment before procurement will go a long way towards the resolution of fundamental operational issues prior to system installation.

The lab also provides a training area for support personnel on a system that is ready for installation. Hands-on training and demonstrations are possible without impacting daily broadcast operations.

Taking care of one's own

CableLabs maintains a laboratory for system development, integration and testing. This includes a certification program for compliant equipment. The CEA also tests and certifies consumer equipment.

There is no similar development, testing and certification system or association for ATSC standards. This leaves the practical application of ATSC standards to vendors and broadcasters to work out.

New standards are continually proposed and adopted as advanced techniques and technologies emerge. Current standards are modified and amended as new production and infrastructure requirements necessitate.

Proposed standards are drafted and refined by Working Groups. When ready for submission to committee members, a Candidate Standard is circulated for review and comment.

The ATSC description of a Candidate Standard reads as follows:

A Candidate Standard is a document that has received significant review within a specialist group. Advancement of a document to Candidate Standard is an explicit call to those outside of the related specialist group for implementation and technical feedback. This is the phase at which the specialist group is responsible for formally acquiring that experience or at least defining the expectations of implementation.

Presentation

Efforts to attain more convincing levels of presentation realism are seemingly never-ending. DTV video and audio presentation continues to evolve to higher video resolutions and refresh rates while surround speaker configurations progress to 6.1, 7.1 and beyond.

1080 60p

Although a 1080 60 Hz progressive video presentation format was desired by the Grand Alliance system designers, technology and cost constraints made this

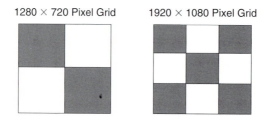

FIGURE 7.1 *1280 × 720 and 1920 × 1080 Equal Area Pixel Grid Comparison. Each box represents one pixel in each format*

impractical in the early 1990s. To attain this goal in the future, a high data rate transport stream mode, at 38.78 Mbps, was specified, even though its use would be limited to acceptable deployment scenarios.

In a reverse twist, consumer DTV manufacturers are producing 1080 60 Hz progressive capable sets which are now driving infrastructure enhancement. The benefit of 1080 60p displays lies more in the fact that the full 1920 active horizontal pixels will be displayed. Early displays used fewer pixels per line.

1080 60p will render current BOC technology insufficient because SMPTE 292 and distribution topologies are based on 1.5 Gbps, single cable distribution. Dual link methods that support 3 Gbps are necessary.

Figure 7.1 compares 720 60p and 1080 60p pixels grids. Each box represents a pixel. As can be seen, three 1080p boxes are equivalent to two 720p boxes in the horizontal direction. The same is true of the vertical direction. Hence, the maximum resolution of 720p is less than 1080p. The difference in size of alternating black and white boxes illustrates the difference in detail resolution between the two formats. 1920 boxes are smaller than 720p boxes and therefore can resolve finer details.

In Figure 7.2, by repeating each of the boxes for both formats, it becomes obvious how the 1080 60p format can resolve finer detail than the 720 60p format in both the horizontal and vertical directions.

Blue Ray and HD-DVDs store content in the 1080 24p or 60i format, not in a native, true 1080 60p format. The display device or disk player uses scaling techniques to up-convert to 60p with the resultant loss in temporal resolution. This can result in visible artifacts.

Upgrading SMPTE 292

To address the need for higher speed infrastructure distribution standards to support 1080 60p, SMPTE has adopted the SMPTE 424 and SMPTE 425, 3 Gbps SDI protocols.

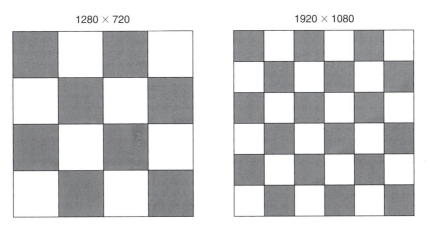

FIGURE 7.2 *720p and 1080p Equal Area Spatial Resolution Comparison. Each box represents one pixel in each display format*

SMPTE 424M-2006, "3 Gb/s Signal/Data Serial Interface," defines a bit-serial transport data structure for 3 Gbs component digital signals or packetized data using a coaxial cable interface.

Beyond 1080 60p

The latest generation of DTV receivers touts 1080 60p displays that present the full 1920 active horizontal pixels (rather than 1366 or some other lower number). The pictures are truly amazing. Even the largest displays produce high fidelity pictures.

But is 1080 60p enough? Digital cinema uses resolutions of 2 K and 4 K. At least one large manufacturer of DTV receivers feels that the home theatre experience will settle on a 2 K display pixel grid. Dolby True-HD and DTS-HD surround sound are uncompressed systems that are supported by HDMI consumer equipment interconnections. These formats are beyond the ability of any current delivery channel's capability.

Will downloads be the only method of delivering content to the home in 2 K and with uncompressed surround sound? Or will a 2 K hard disk recording capability give the movie industry a unique level of quality for home consumption of theatrical productions? The movie industry works in 2 K and 4 K production formats and may be the only source form these super high resolution formats.

If the consumer home theatre environment moves to 2 K and HD audio, broadcasters will be hard pressed to match the experience that digital cinema may be able to deliver in the home.

A companion standard, SMPTE 425M-2006, "3 Gb/s Signal/Data Serial Interface — Source Image Format Mapping," specifies the mapping of various source image formats, the carriage of embedded audio, ancillary data and stream ID, in a 3 Gbs serial digital interface. It also specifies a method for mapping two SMPTE 292 M HD SDI interfaces including SMPTE 372 M, Dual Link 292 M Interface for 1920×1080 Picture Raster, into a serial digital interface operating at a rate of 3 Gbs.

Graphics cards support dual link distribution methodology. Broadcast infrastructures will have to adapt their existing HD SDI distribution infrastructure to support 1080 60p over a dual link 3 Gbps channel.

VANC and HANC

As more and more metadata is conveyed in the ancillary data area of an SDI signal, and as the associated content is both encoded for transmission and archived for future use, persistence of this information in an MXF file (or another appropriate format) becomes a desired capability. Techniques of storing VBI information, such as closed captioning and production control instructions, can simplify workflows and automate production processes.

SMPTE 436 M-2006, "MXF Mappings for VBI Lines and Ancillary Data Packets," describes the carriage of VBI data and ANC packets (HANC and VANC) in an MXF file. This standard also defines the encoding of additional information so an MXF decoder can place the VBI data and ANC packets at the specified location in a reconstructed television signal.

Compression

One aspect that is representative of the elegance of the system design of the Grand Alliance DTV architecture is subsystem modularity and a tool kit approach. This approach is enabling the development and eventual use of more powerful audio and video encoders that produce lower data rates for quality that is comparable to MPEG-2 and AC-3 compression.

The benefit of any of these emerging compression methodologies is the reduction of data (bit) rates for a given level of audio or video quality. As presentation devices, displays and surround sound systems improve in resolution and fidelity, compression artifacts become noticeable. Hence, better compression algorithms will support a more realistic DTV experience.

MPEG-4

MPEG has continued its work in audio and video compression with MPEG-4. While earlier methods of MPEG compression divided the video pixel grid into fixed sized blocks of pixels, MPEG-4 has added an object-oriented paradigm to the compression tool kit. These items are:

- Video Object

- Still Object

- Mesh Object

- Face and Body Animation Object

By breaking a scene down into background and foreground objects, each can be coded separately. This technique is known as texture coding.

Another MPEG-4 method, reminiscent of early augmentation channel NSTC compatible HDTV systems, is defining a base-level bitstream at a given frame rate and providing additional information that can be used to create a higher frame rate. An application of this tool could be used in producing video that scales to the highest attainable quality dependent on the data capacity of the delivery channel.

Animation is enabled by applying vector information to still faces and bodies. This ultimately requires less data than coding motion as differences in video frames.

An MPEG-4 decoder is somewhat akin to a render engine. The shapes and textures described in the encoding process are reconstructed into a video frame in real-time. MPEG-4 also is able to interface to proprietary DRM systems and other Intellectual Property Management and Protection (IPMP) systems.

However, MPEG-4 Part 10 has been the focus of much attention due to its improved video compression efficiency. This has eclipsed implementation of many other parts of MPEG-4. MPEG-4 Part 10, known as Advanced Video Coding (AVC) and based on ITU H.264, is under consideration as a video compression standard by SMPTE, SCTE and the ATSC. The SCTE standard to define constraints and transport of AVC is approaching the formal approval stage.

VC-1

Since the late 1990s, Microsoft has attempted to make inroads into the television industry. Their first effort called for the convergence of all media storage and consumption devices to be centered around a PC. Microsoft's vision has evolved and the success of Windows Media codecs has led to an unprecedented action: Windows Media video compression (Video Codec 1) technology and transport have been submitted to SMPTE and the ATSC for consideration as standards.

SMPTE 421M-2006, "VC-1 Compressed Video Bitstream Format and Decoding Process," defines the bitstream syntax and semantics for compressed video data in VC-1 format. The complete process required to decode the bitstream is described. Video formats supported by VC-1 include progressive and interlaced. The decoding process outputs 8-bits per component video sample corresponding to the original 4:2:0 sampling grid. Microsoft, in conjunction with the SMPTE standardization of Windows Media/VC-1, offers a DRM suite.

The ATSC has posted a Candidate Standard covering the coding constraints for VC-1 use in ATSC streams.

Enhanced-AC-3

In the never-ending quest for more features and lower data rates, Dolby has developed Dolby Plus. The technology has been standardized as Enhanced AC-3 (E-AC-3) and is one of the normative optional annexes of ATSC A/52. Annex E, "Enhanced AC-3 Bit Stream Syntax," specifies syntax extensions that support additional coding tools and features.

New capabilities of E-AC-3 include up to 13.1 audio channels, coding tools that produce lower bits rates and a "fall-back" capability when used with E-VSB (discussed later in this chapter).

It is important to note that E-AC-3 is not backward-compatible with AC-3, so an AC-3 decoder cannot process E-AC-3. Instead, a partial decode of an E-AC-3 stream and an encoding to AC-3 is necessary. Because of common attributes, a complete decode and encode is not necessary.

MPEG Advanced Audio Coding

MPEG working groups have not left audio behind. Advanced Audio Coding (AAC) was developed as part of MPEG-2 and now forms the basis for MPEG-4 audio tools.

AAC is not backward compatible with earlier MPEG audio techniques. It supports up to 48 audio channels. Similar to MPEG-2 video, it offers a choice of coding levels based on complexity. Lossless coding tools are available.

MPEG-4 ACC adds Perceptual Noise Substitution (PNS) and vector quantization. PNS is a technique where the encoder does not attempt to encode audio noise. Since noise is random, predictive techniques cannot be used to reduce the amount of data produced by compression. Instead, based on a psychoaural model, noise that cannot be distinguished as sound or circuit noise is ignored and not compressed.

Vector quantization, is also called block quantization, and does not use Huffman coding (see Chapter 2) on each individual coefficient. Instead, the method translates blocks of coefficients into a symbol.

Delivery and Distribution

In response to concerns about high variability among transport stream monitoring equipment implementations, the ATSC has issued a recommended practice to provide guidance about what matters most and least when monitoring streams that "officially" should comply with A/53 and A/65.

Issued in September 2006, A/78, "ATSC Recommended Practice: Transport Stream Verification", provides a common methodology for describing TS conformance criteria and explicitly describes the elements and parameters of A/53 and A/65 that should be verified in an ATSC TS for it to be considered a proper emission. The ATSC document incorporates a DVB standard (ETSI TR 101 290) and makes distinctions among types of errors, ranging from those that are not expected to have any impact to those that mean the stream is essentially useless.

Enhanced VSB

Addressing criticisms of 8-VSB demodulation performance, the ATSC has adopted an Enhanced VSB (E-VSB) standard that adds extra error correction to the 8-VSB signal. Enhanced data and additional forward error correction modify some of the packets that would be used as 8-VSB symbols.

Reed Solomon coding and trellis coding parameters have been altered. This enhanced data is encapsulated into transport packets. A convolutional coder has been inserted in the enhanced processing stream. The entire E-VSB process is transparent to an 8-VSB decoder and the enhanced data packets will be ignored.

The E-VSB transmission mode is described in A/53D Annex D. Specification of advanced video codecs for use in the E-VSB mode, defining the video system characteristics for VC-1 and AVC, are published as Candidate Standards. They include how CEA-708-B closed captions are to be carried with either codec.

Use of either of these new video codecs, in addition to MPEG-2, in the E-VSB mode, will require extensions to transport specification and would be documented as an amendment to A/53.

It is envisioned that these enhanced capabilities will enable transmission of additional streams. This may enable mobile applications that require more robust error correction than 8-VSB.

The enhanced methodology also enables a "fall-back" scenario. Under difficult transmission environments, when data is corrupted beyond recovery, lower bit rate audio and video can be encoded and successfully transmitted and decoded. PSIP data would announce the presence of fall-back information to an enhanced-capable DTV receiver.

ATSC Satellite Standards

The ATSC has issued satellite delivery specifications. They are based on the DVB EN 300 421 satellite standard framing structure, channel coding and modulation techniques.

A/80, "Modulation and Coding Requirements for Digital TV (DTV) Applications Over Satellite," defines a standard for modulation and coding of data delivered over satellite for DTV contribution and distribution applications. The data can be a collection of program material including video, audio, data or multimedia. QPSK, 8PSK and 16 QAM modulation modes are included, as well as a range of forward error correction techniques.

A/81, "Direct-to-Home Satellite Broadcast Standard," describes the emission system for an ATSC Direct-to-Home (DTH) Satellite Broadcast System. Extensions to audio, video, transport and PSIP subsystems as well carriage of data broadcasting as defined in ATSC Standard A/90 are specified.

ATSC Distributed Transmission

Traditional analog broadcasting uses one transmitter and a single frequency per channel. The geographic area covered by this signal has formed the basis of DMAs that have been the foundation of television's advertising-based revenue model.

DTV frequency allocations have striven to maintain the same distribution contours as the original analog channels. Because of differences in digital modulation and emission characteristics, this has not always been possible to attain at acceptable power levels. The result is significant co-channel interference.

By using multiple distributed transmitters at lower power levels, DTV transmissions can minimize co-channel interference and maintain DMA coverage. This technique is called a Distributed Transmission Network (DTxN). Implementations can be a Single Frequency Network (SFN) or a Multiple Frequency Network (MFN).

There are three types of multiple transmitter deployments: Distributed-Transmitter Network, Distributed-Translator Network and Digital On-Channel Repeater (DOCR).

The ATSC has produced a standard and a recommended practice to guide engineers in design and deployment of compliant DTxNs.

A/110A, "Synchronization Standard for Distributed Transmission, Revision A," defines a standard for synchronization of multiple transmitters emitting trellis coded 8-VSB signals in accordance with ATSC A/53 Annex D (RF/Transmission Systems Characteristics). The document specifies mechanisms necessary to transmit synchronization signals to several transmitters using a dedicated PID value, including the formatting of packets associated with that PID and without altering the signal format emitted from the transmitters.

A/111, "Design of Synchronized Multiple Transmitter Networks," a recommended practice, examines the types of transmitters used in SFNs and MFNs. The document also concentrates on design aspects of SFNs.

The benefits of DTxN include filling gaps in signal coverage. Reception can be improved in areas that produce multipath reflections, such as cities. SFNs can be used to replace a single transmitter.

MPEG and Metadata

Although the original focus of MPEG work was on audio and video systems, the scope of present MPEG standards development has moved beyond presentation, compression and transport. Recognizing the role of metadata in content and rights management, MPEG committees are developing methods and techniques to ease the transition to metadata-enabled, automated and interoperable content management systems.

MPEG-7

MPEG-7 is a standard for content description and provides a standardized mechanism for describing signal features as well as content structure. MPEG-4 and MPEG-7 are intended to work in a complementary fashion.

Facilitating automated interoperable search, retrieval and management of content is a motivating design goal of MPEG-7. XML is used to define content at a high level of abstraction. It is important to note that only the format of content descriptions is specified. How to encode, decode and use the techniques described in the standard is left to the user of the MPEG-7 tools.

Metadata definitions can be categorized as:

- Description Definition Language (DDL)

- Multimedia Description Language (MDL)

- Audio and Visual Metadata Definitions

Content management systems based on MPEG-7 are now offered by content management systems vendors and are beginning to be used in broadcast operation centers.

MPEG-21

MPEG-21 Multimedia Framework seeks to establish interoperability between devices without the limitations of incompatible media formats, codecs and metadata. Users interact with digital items—the content and the description.

Users have control over access to their content consumption history. This is important in restricting access by unauthorized parties to personal consumption information when implementing interactive DTV capabilities.

The fundamental description of an object used in AAF is paralleled by MPEG-21 and is called a digital item. It consists of content and a description of the content. Digital Broadcast Items (DBI) are logical units that express the relationship of content elements that are intended for broadcast.

A rose is a rose...

The attentive reader will notice that MPEG-21 and the SMPTE Task Force are using different terms to express identical concepts.

MPEG-21: Digital Item = Content + Description

SMPTE: Content = Essence + Metadata

Once again, this underscores the care that must be taken in using technical terms in their proper context.

XML is used to specify the Digital Item Declaration, Digital Item Identification and Description. These components provide a means to uniquely identify content and a way to locate its associated rights information.

At the heart of MPEG-21 are the Rights Expression Language (REL) and Rights Data Dictionary (RDD). The REL and RDD express rights in a standardized, interchangeable form using a defined terminology.

As expressed by the REL, the creator assigns usage rights to entities that have certain, defined things they can do with these rights. These rights are specified in a license. A "principal" can give or retain rights. Principals are authorized to copy, edit, transform and perform other actions on content.

Enhanced, Interactive and Personalized

Broadcasting and content consumption has always been a one-way passive activity. What you see is what you get. From the Golden Age of television, when just seeing a picture was spellbinding, through the decades with ever more sophisticated graphics and special effects, to the present where picture content frequently occupies a minority area of the screen, all these "enhancements" have been done in the quest to provide the viewer with as much "useful" information as possible.

Some feel that this visual information deluge is beyond usable to the point of distraction. Ever watch a news show, catch a glimpse of something on the crawl, and then be glued to the crawl, to the elimination of awareness of the program, waiting until the crawl item reappears? By then you've missed what you were originally watching. Although multitasking is a fashionable phrase, is does not always facilitate depth of comprehension.

DTV standards exist that, when properly implemented, will allow a viewer to control the presence and appearance of supplemental information. Graphic overlays could be turned on and off. Snipes and distracting programming alerts that have invaded shows while they are being broadcast may be permitted or denied like Internet pop-ups. Personalized features that enable parsing a news crawl for specific information, something like an RSS feed, will alert the viewer to the availability of requested information.

> Snipes are corner animations used to tease a viewer into upcoming shows. The term has been used in the print media industry to describe the area where a magazine uses a triangular corner of a cover page to add extra information in an eye catching manner.

With enhanced, interactive and personalized features, broadcasting may move into a permission-based content delivery and presentation model. Resourceful, innovative business development managers will find ways to use these new, user-controlled capabilities to build brand loyalty. In an ideal situation, viewers could begin to ask for more program content or commercial information about an advertiser's product or service.

Video On Demand (VOD) and Pay Per View (PPV) applications are leading the way. The significance of VOD and PPV are not just that these applications have opened the door to new revenue sources. They also have introduced an infrastructure that paves the way for future enhanced, interactive and personalized features and services.

For VOD and PPV, a bi-directional communication infrastructure is necessary to implement the business model and automate billing. An option to receive content is presented to a consumer. The consumer selects the content they want delivered. A request message is sent back to the content provider. The content is delivered and the customer is billed. The entire process is automated. These steps are the basic building blocks for more sophisticated enhanced, interactive and personalized DTV applications.

Enabling Standards

DASE (DTV Application Suite Environment) was the initial ATSC enhanced TV enabling standard. OCAP (Open Cable Application Protocol) is the CableLabs specification for iTV. The Multimedia Home Protocol (MHP) is the ITU technical specification for iTV/eTV implementation.

ATSC A/101, the "Advanced Common Application Platform (ACAP)," is intended to be used in writing terminal specifications and/or standards based on ACAP and by developers of applications that use the ACAP functionality and APIs. ACAP aims to ensure interoperability between ACAP applications and different implementations of platforms supporting ACAP applications. ACAP harmonizes DASE and OCAP.

An ACAP application is information which is processed by software and enables interaction with an end-user. In short, it enables enhanced and interactive DTV capabilities. The presence of ACAP data must be signaled in the transport stream. A/102, "ACAP Service Signaling and Announcement," augments MPEG-2 transport signaling as specified in A/101. The document defines methods for signaling the presence of current services and for the announcement of future services.

Interactivity meets DTV

Samsung developed the first ACAP/OCAP-ready HDTV. An ACAP system (in conjunction with Aircode) was demonstrated in the DTV Drafthouse at NAB 2004. STBs manufactured by Motorola and Scientific-Atlanta are OCAP-capable. An inspection of these boxes reveals RJ-45 network, Firewire and other interfaces. How far away is TV/PC network connectivity? What will be the killer app to drive the home network implementation of these communication portals?

A DTV receiver really is a digital signal processing computer running software applications. Enhanced and interactive TV features are enabled by software applications. Contemporary programming languages and toolkits have been extended to address ACAP, OCAP and MHP development.

ACAP applications are classified into two categories depending upon whether the initial application content processed is of a procedural or a declarative nature. These categories of applications are referred to as procedural (ACAP-J) and declarative (ACAP-X) applications.

Back Channels

Two-way communication must be present to implement truly interactive TV. A means for the viewer to communicate with the content originator or service provider is necessary and is referred to as the "back channel." Figure 7.3 illustrates the capabilities of various content delivery channels to facilitate upstream communication via a back channel.

Satellite and OTA broadcasters have limited choices for implementing back channel capabilities. There really is just one practical method—the Internet.

Initial cable system deployments were one-way, downstream delivery of television programs. To take advantage of the business opportunity available by implementing broadband Internet services, cable operators have made considerable financial investments and upgraded their plants to two-way communication capability.

When OTA programming is delivered by cable operators, any consumer with broadband Internet cable can reach a broadcaster via the Web. Those without cable will have to use DSL or a dial-up modem.

An alternate method that provides limited upstream communication is the use of cell phones and home phones. Don't underestimate the potential of this interactive method. In 2006, a viewer participation show garnered over 45 million phone votes.

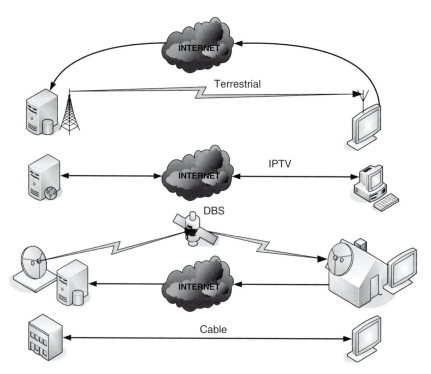

FIGURE 7.3 *Content Distribution and Back Channel Scenarios*

eTV and iTV Implementation

The distinction between interactive TV (iTV) and enhanced TV (eTV) is that iTV has an active means of communicating back to the content provider, while eTV features are dependent on content and data that has been delivered to the STB or DTV receiver. Basically, iTV has two-way communication capabilities, while eTV may appear to be interactive, "pseudo interactive," but all content and data has been downloaded arbitrarily.

Screen scenarios

Interactivity can be thought of as either a one- or two-screen scenario. A one screen implementation uses only the DTV for interactivity. Using the remote, a consumer can click an icon to see more information, to purchase an item, etc. The two-screen scenario requires a DTV and a PC. The PC uses its Internet connection to facilitate the consumer's desired activity.

An alternative is a display that can accept DTV and PC input and simultaneously present windows for each signal source. Ambitious technophiles will implement this method until the DTV/PC convergence is complete.

Content Creation

New authoring tools are necessary to create content that will be used in eTV and iTV applications. The content and extra eTV/iTV data must be formatted and edited for the intended application and presentation platform. Communication and synchronization information needs to be incorporated in the transport stream data. Authoring tools for creating eTV and iTV content are offered by turn-key system vendors.

Targeted DTV Advertising

Targeting potentially responsive consumers has always been the goal of commercial advertising in any medium. But the yield per dollar is small and difficult to quantify. An old ad industry adage says, "I know I am reaching half of my audience; I just don't know which half."

Cable operators and IPTV service providers are already using targeted advertising. Traditional broadcasters must adapt.

Two key interdependent issues, personalization and privacy, must be resolved before enhanced and interactive DTV can be enjoyed by the masses. In order to personalize DTV, viewer profiles must be made available to content providers. However, freely distributing personal information can lead to privacy concerns. Using MPEG-21 could allow the consumer to maintain control over their personal data.

Personalization

The custom publishing segment of the magazine industry uses database-marketing techniques to personalize content and target customers. Based on one-to-one marketing principals, evangelized by Peppers and Rogers, the methodology builds a trusting relationship with its best customers and delivers permission-based, targeted personalized content.

Targeted DTV advertising (also called addressable advertising) will bring one-to-one marketing principles to the television industry. Content and ads will be suggested or delivered to a defined target audience based on demographics, psychographics, geographic location, viewing habits, previous viewing choices, ad response and any other relevant distinguishing characteristics that are permitted to be gathered.

Privacy

In order to target advertising, a viewer profile must be kept. Where a viewer profile is stored and the delivery channel (OTA, cable or DBS) used, directly impacts the security of personal information.

In OTA and DBS systems, without a backchannel, it would be safe to have a user enter and store in their DTV whatever personal information they deem necessary to get the ad they would like. Let's a say you wanted ads about cars. Entering the keyword "CAR" in your receive filtering criteria would enable car ads to get through the firewall.

To enable targeted advertising features in a one-way communication channel, the viewer will have to create a DTV user profile. So to opt-in, ZIP code and other information must be entered. Unlike two-way systems, this information will remain confidential, because there is no way for the content originator to access this personal data in a unidirectional ACAP implementation.

In cable system OCAP implementations, the backchannel is innate to the system technology. A viewer's personal profile, viewing habits and history can be stored in an OCAP-enabled STB in a similar fashion to the way a cookie stores data about its user on the computer. The MSO would have access to this data and could determine demographic and psychographic groups. The MSO sells the demo to the ad client, and the media buyer handles the implementation details of directing the addressable ad to the target viewers in the desired group. The advertiser never has viewer information.

In theory (but not yet deployed in consumer devices) triggers can be enabled by viewer profile information to determine what version of an ad will be shown and how it will be personalized. Cable MSOs may very well the first to deploy STBs with this capability.

Targeted Ad Creation and Delivery

Targeted advertising technology and services providers offer end-to-end systems that include authoring, production tools and a cable system distribution infrastructure. Two fundamental targeting methods are:

- For a 30-second spot, the first 25 seconds are identical everywhere and the final five feature a personalized tag.

- Runs different ad content simultaneously. Targeted demo based options are inserted through out the commercial.

An example of a personalized tag is when the first 25 seconds talks about the wonderful features of a specific car and the last five seconds communicates the nearest location where the car can be purchased. The other method, based on personalized information, can identify a rugged outdoorsy person and shows SUV commercials instead of two-seater roadsters.

As the commercial is storyboarded, decisions are made as to when to insert targeted segments. A determination is made as to whether the customized segments

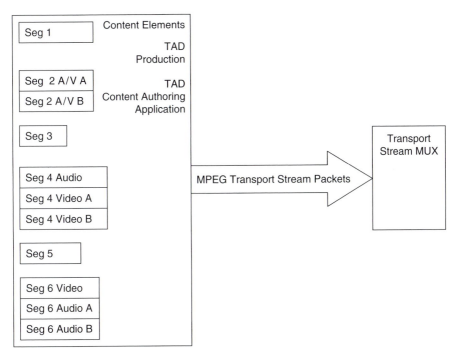

FIGURE 7.4 *Targeted Ad Preparation*

should contain common or targeted audio, video or graphics. In Figure 7.4, segments 1, 3 and 5 are consistent for the two possible versions, while segment 2 has the option of two completely different audio/video components. In segment 4, the audio is consistent with two video options, and segment 6 is the reverse—two audio options with a common video segment.

When the spot runs, viewer demographics are read by a DTV receiver or STB application. As the elements of the commercial are presented, instructions determine which audio, video or graphics (contained in unique PID packets) should be presented based on the viewer profile.

The Bottom Line

Advertisers, consumers and broadcasters all will profit from targeted television advertising. The advertiser reaches the optimum number of potential customers and the viewer gets more relevant information than is possible with a one-size-fits-all commercial.

Taking Aim

Identifying which programs should deliver targeted ad content is important. At least one media buying tool is a recommender application for selection of TV shows that fit the target demo an advertiser is trying to reach. This allows double targeting, delivering a given age/gender demo (18–34 year old males) and then further dividing by another qualifier (such as ZIP code).

Broadcasters can increase revenue by charging for enhanced targeted advertising delivery services. Data mining, analysis and demographic breakdown by a broadcaster can become a new, billable service included as part of the ad sale process. The billing rationale is to realize a ROI in equipment necessary to provide this targeted capability.

Implementation

Fundamental to any eTV or iTV implementation is the capability to insert data into a transport stream. Data transport packets with a unique PID are delivered to the decoder and enter the data carousel, which holds data and makes particular information available to a user on a cyclic basis.

Triggers are enabled by viewer info and determine what and where the ad will be personalized. For example, click a button on the remote and a window pops up!

Pseudo Interactive eTV

Without a backchannel, an illusion of interactivity can be implemented using the potential of the data carousel. Possible features include:

- Telescoping ads take the viewer to successively detailed information

- Personalization triggers alert the viewer only to the presence of information they have requested

- Turning off the clock, score and bottom line to watch just an HDTV sports presentation

Figure 7.5 illustrates a telescoping ad using the data carousel technique in an eTV (no back channel) scenario. One-way downstream communication limits data to that provided by the broadcaster without any input from the content consumer.

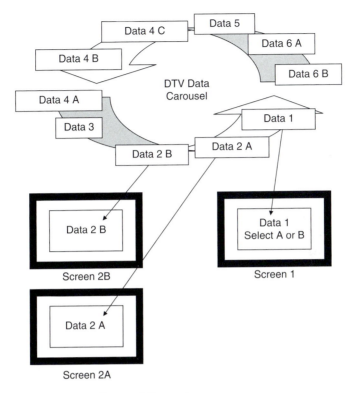

FIGURE 7.5 *eTV Data Carousel Scenario*

All data elements are delivered opportunistically to the DTV receiver and "circulate" on the data carousel. An announcement (Data 1) signals the viewer that additional information is available. Selecting either A or B, the next screen of information (Data 2A or Data 2B) is presented.

In an iTV environment, as shown in Figure 7.6, data elements are downloaded by viewer requests transferred to the content provider via the back channel. Two-way communication enables the content consumer to request the information to be sent by the broadcaster offering many variable options. The data carousel can be used as a buffer.

Because of the lack of two-way communication, eTV implementations are less flexible than iTV. Relevant data must be predicted and the amount that can be delivered is limited with eTV. iTV is flexible and can deliver virtually unlimited information by request.

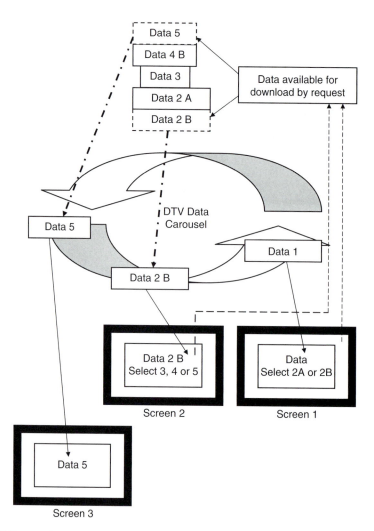

FIGURE 7.6 *iTV Data Carousel Scenario*

Directed Channel Change

Another method that can facilitate eTV features for OTA and satellite broadcasters is the Directed Channel Change (DCC) capability. Based on a viewer profile or at the request of the viewer, the DCC can force the DTV receiver to switch to a demographically relevant ad on a multicast channel. Broadcasters can offer (at an additional rate) use of their auxiliary bandwidth (extra SD channel or HD data pipe) for additional commercial information that can be requested by the viewer.

iTV and the Internet

As broadcasters attempt to implement iTV features that consumers will utilize in a way that increases revenue, there is a growing threat from the Internet. Users are completely at ease with the interactivity of the Internet. Connection speeds are increasing rapidly. If DTV, especially HDTV, can be delivered over this existing infrastructure, an iTV experience will be innate.

Is there a broadcaster left that does not have a Web site? Production and transmission infrastructure efficiencies can be leveraged for multiplatform delivery. Just how you tell a compelling story on each platform remains to be established, but if the trend to home digital media networks continues, the delivery method will be a moot point. Any signal source that enters the home can be directed to any display or playback device. Broadcasters would be wise to prepare for all possible delivery options.

eTV, iTV and Personalized Applications

eTV and iTV features are being implemented now. Granted, they are in their infancy, but sooner or later, a killer app is bound to be discovered.

Sports implementations could enable customers to receive stats and scores from professional and college teams. Other features include alerts that give the viewer the option to switch to important action in other games, game replays and "mosaic" display of multiple games in individual windows on a single screen.

Localized features can be based on ZIP codes. A user profile, similar to that used on the Internet and including a 4-digit PIN, is entered into a DTV or STB.

A VOD methodology can be used to enhance advertising delivery and offer an on demand advertising platform.

Another approach that enables targeted content delivery seeds STBs with demographic and behavioral statistics within specific groups. This data is then used by each STB to parse incoming content and switch to the most relevant information based on stored data.

Some companies are examining the convergence of TV and PC by evaluating PC-based ACAP middleware receivers. TV commerce, educational datacasting and viewer polling are among the applications being tested.

Broadcasters, consumers and advertisers all profit from personalization and interactivity. The viewer is in control and gets relevant content and information.

A global perspective

The United States may have won the race to deploy HD and DTV, but the rest of the world is ahead in enhanced and interactive TV deployments.

The Korean Broadcast System has been active in developing eTV and iTV. Efforts with DASE and ACAP-enabled features are now being implemented. A DBS operator has deployed more than one million MHP-enabled DBS iTV STBs since 2001. Services offered include weather, news, horoscopes, traffic and educational information.

Numerous European countries have also deployed eTV and iTV applications. In Great Britain, BBC Interactive offers Freeview interactivity on OTA, cable and satellite systems. At any time, viewers can press a button to jump to interactive content and features.

German broadcasters have rolled out MHP-based interactive services. In Italy, 1.5 million MHP-enabled receivers for digital terrestrial TV have been sold. An interactive OTA MHP data service channel is available in Spain. Several broadcasters in Finland also provide OTA, cable and DBS enhanced and interactive services.

Televisia in Mexico has constructed a PSI/PSIP/iTV system. Initial ACAP tests were successful in broadcasting to several reception sites.

The advertiser reaches the optimum number of potential customers and increases ROI. Broadcasters satisfy their viewers by placing them in control of their TV experience and advertisers by delivering more lift for their investment. Charging for personalized and enhanced delivery services can increase revenue.

Proceed with Caution

Several lessons should be learned from the mistakes of the Internet. From the outset, both content creator's rights and viewer's privacy should be protected. The opt-out model should be replaced with an opt-in choice to participate approach.

With these "Web-like" iTV features, a legal restriction on TV spam is important. Pop-ups are annoying on a PC but will be intolerable to a TV viewer. FCC regulations and other legal restrictions must be enacted to stop the flow of unwanted TV spam before it can begin.

The ad industry must be wary of killing the goose that laid the golden egg. If the ability to download ad content is abused, consumers will not want sets with iTV and eTV features.

In addition, security must be iron-clad to prevent identity theft during "T-commerce" and from transaction and user profile databases.

Virtual Product Placement

All sports fans have become used to the first and ten yellow line and strike zone effects. Produced by sophisticated real-time processing engines, they have enhanced our understanding and enjoyment of sports broadcasts. Similar technology now enables the inclusion of virtual advertising in programs. Using this technique, a broadcaster can insert a commercial graphic as part of the scene.

Virtual billboards are at a first generation implementation stage. In sports, a playing field may have a billboard inserted at times of inaction. This feature can be expanded significantly. A step beyond product placement, if coupled with behavioral technology, a broadcaster may target and customize these virtual ads based on consumer demographics and habits. iTV capabilities can be exploited by enabling the consumer to request more product info by clicking on the virtual ad/product.

Multiplatform Emergency Alert System

As the broadcast industry transitions to digital, the Emergency Alert System (EAS) is undergoing a transformation. Faced with the loss of the television segment of the EAS when NTSC is shutdown, the FCC has adopted DTV requirements that mandate broadcast of DTV EAS messages.

FEMA, as part of the Department of Homeland Security, now has jurisdiction over the EAS. The FCC defines technical standards and operational rules and enforces broadcaster compliance with EAS requirements.

The EAS transmission pathways consist of a network of radio relay stations, the "EAS web." Thirty-four radio stations are designated as national Primary Entry Points (PEP). PEP facilities are radiation-hardened and intended to continue operating in the event of a nuclear blast. They have a National Primary (NP) designation and are monitored by Local Primary 1 (LP-1) stations other stations.

At the request of the President, FEMA distributes "Presidential Level" messages to the PEP stations. At the state level, a governor may initiate an emergency message. Similarly, a request for activation on the local level is directed to the LP.

What's the Problem?

Studies of the EAS system have found that the relay system does not function reliably. With daisy chain transmission paths, a failure at one station will cause a failure in the rest of the relay chain.

Operator error can produce erroneous alerts. A radiological warning and an Emergency Alert Notification (EAN), reserved for Presidential communications at a time of extreme national emergency, have been erroneously activated!

Low-quality technical implementations that result in unintelligible communications from limited bandwidth audio systems render an alert useless. Failure to identify an alert or dead air during insertion will encourage channel surfing and the message will be missed.

Other concerns and criticisms are diminishing funds, system security, lack of mandatory participation on the state and local level, failure to require alerts to be relayed and doubt as to whether the EAS itself could survive an attack.

Interoperability

Cell phones, PDAs and the Internet offer many personalized alerts and notification services. It is logical that discussion has turned to a multiplatform updating of the EAS.

Creation of EAS interoperability standards will ensure that emergency warning systems can communicate with each other. This will allow first responders, emergency and event managers, public health agency officials, and executive management in the public and private sectors to share critical information during an emergency or major event. And most importantly, to communicate messages in a timely manner, in a meaningful way that is understood by all.

Common Alerting Protocol (CAP) is an open standard for the exchange of emergency alerts and public warning over data networks, computer-controlled public warning systems, and emergency management software applications. CAP allows a consistent warning message to be disseminated simultaneously over many different warning systems, thus increasing warning effectiveness while simplifying the alerting task. Using CAP, emergency responders can:

- Ensure alert messages reach the right audience at the right time
- Reduce the workload and costs associated with multiple warning systems
- Enhance technical reliability

- Ensure consistency in the information transmitted over multiple delivery systems

- Reduce costs and operational complexities by eliminating the need for multiple custom interfaces to warning sources and dissemination systems

In August 2003, the EIC released a draft of the CAP by the OASIS Emergency Management Technical Committee. In April 2004, CAP version 1.0 was adopted as a full OASIS www.oasis-open.org standard.

The Multiplatform EAS Future

Recommendations for upgrading the EAS system include the following features and requirements:

- Mandatory compliance for all EAS, NWS, All-Hazard and AMBER alerts on state and local levels and must relay all alerts

- Use of the Common Alert Protocol (CAP)

- Redundant delivery platforms such as TV, cable, satellite, AM/FM/digital radio, the Internet, cell phones and PDAs

- Development of TVs and other devices that turn on or change channels for a relevant EAS message

The 2005 tsunami painfully pointed out that, even with the existent sophisticated communication networks, a timely warning was not issued. Something as trivial knowing who to call could possibly have saved many lives. The United Nations is attempting to establish a global system to predict disasters. The International Early Warning Program (IEWP, www.unisdr.org/ppew) is an effort to establish a global emergency alert system.

In the U.S., Congressional bills implement 9/11 Commission recommendations and require a study of the feasibility of implementing an "emergency telephonic alert notifications system" and call for the creation of a "READICALL" emergency alert system. A pilot study using network technology to improve public warning systems is also proposed.

Transition to digital technologies and an all-hazard EAS system is the future. A test deployment, to be implemented by PBS stations (including WETA and Maryland Public TV), DHS, NOAA and the FCC is planned for Washington, D.C., in 2007. Figure 7.7 demonstrates how multiplatform EAS deployment would reach the general public through many channels.

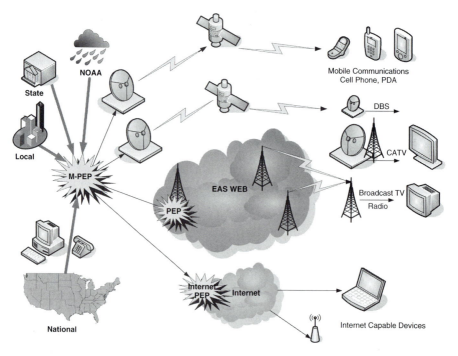

FIGURE 7.7 *Multiplatform EAS Deployment*

Summary

- New standards influence the future. New technology influences standards. Both influence new business models.

- A shift from reactive standards setting, endorsing a manufacturer's technology, to proactive, all industry participation is becoming the standards-setting methodology.

- There is a trend towards higher audio and video presentation resolution, higher compression ratios with new codecs, transport stream enabled eTV and iTV and transmission error concealment enhancements.

- DTV offers the opportunity to personalize content consumption, as well as implement enhanced and interactive features.

- The transition to digital that began with the ATSC standard and continued with the conversion of the BOC infrastructure. It will conclude with the personal home digital network where the converged TV and PC will be one.

8 The Future and Digital Broadcasting

The DTV transition is no longer about converting to a digital transmission infrastructure. Television "broadcasting" is now about producing and delivering content over every possible delivery channel to any consumer device, anywhere for consumption at any time.

As of late 2006, virtually every television station in the U.S. is broadcasting some format of DTV. It is now time for the industry to look forward to the end of NTSC and the long-awaited surrender of unused spectrum and to plan for the all-digital future of broadcasting.

Three factors will affect DTV in the coming years. First, and probably foremost, is the impact of government regulation. Second, technology will shape implementation of digital broadcasting and determine if the convergence of TV and personal computers will reach completion. And in the end, consumers will vote with their dollars for the features and services that DTV will deliver.

Government Involvement in the Transition

In the U.S., HD and DTV were originally conceived of as an OTA transmission system. Hence, the development of HD and DTV has been heavily influenced by the federal government based on their right to manage the public airwaves. Some will argue that the entire transition to digital broadcasting has been forced upon the television industry. In any event, Congress, the executive and judicial branches, and the FCC will all continue to impact DTV.

Congress

When Congress established the Federal Communications Commission in 1934 as the successor to the Federal Radio Commission, the federal government confirmed its authority to regulate the broadcasting industry. The FCC has continued to assert its authority in many ways since then. From the breaking up of NBC in the 1950s, through indecency statutes, ownership rules and must-carry regulations, Congress, its agencies and the FCC determine the present and future direction of the broadcast business.

As early as 1987, the FCC recognized that a second channel would be necessary for NTSC-compatible HDTV or for simulcast HDTV. As directed by Congress, a plan for the transition to "Advanced TV" loaned each existing broadcaster a new 6 MHz block of spectrum within the same frequency ranges as the existing NTSC channels to transmit ATV signals.

Once the DTV standard was adopted, exactly when the analog spectrum should be returned for auction and what revenue the sale of this spectrum might generate became a hot topic. Predictions from $30 billion to more than $100 billion have been estimated as the take from spectrum auctions.

The Senate Committee on Commerce, Science and Transportation and the House Committee on Energy and Commerce have been extremely active in influencing the course of the development and rollout of DTV. Many committee sessions and public proceedings about ATV have been held over the years.

The Federal Communications Commission

It is possible that the FCC has been more influential than Congress and its committees in the unfolding of the DTV story. They have been on the front lines, defining system requirements, overseeing prototype testing and endorsing the ATSC standard.

The FCC is the federal regulatory body charged with regulating interstate and international communications by radio, television, wire, satellite and cable. The FCC's jurisdiction covers the 50 states, the District of Columbia, and U.S. possessions.

The commission is composed of five members appointed by the President and confirmed by the Senate. One of the members serves as chairman. The FCC reports directly to Congress.

Among the FCC's responsibilities is the issuing of licenses for terrestrial OTA radio and television broadcasters. Each station's license specifies technical parameters such as operating frequency; power output; and type, height and location of the antenna. Station inspections are conducted and fines are levied for noncompliance.

It took 62 years until the Telecommunications Act of 1996 rewrote the Communications Act of 1934. Its thrust was deregulation of the industry. It also forced telephone companies to share their local lines. Many media ownership restrictions were removed and led to consolidation into a few conglomerates. Yet, somewhat ironically, the fundamental motive of the act was to promote competition.

Offices and Bureaus

The FCC is organized into offices and bureaus that address areas of importance to communications.

The Office of Legislative Affairs (OLA) is the FCC's liaison with Congress. It provides lawmakers with information about FCC regulations and prepares FCC witnesses for Congressional hearings.

The Office of Engineering and Technology (OET) advises the Commission concerning engineering matters. Its role is to manage the electromagnetic spectrum and conduct technical studies of advanced terrestrial and space communications. It also organizes the Technical Advisory Council, a committee of advisors from major telecommunication and media corporations, and operates the Equipment Authorization Branch.

The Office of Media Relations (OMR) is responsible for dissemination of Commission announcements, orders, proceedings, and other information per media requests and for managing the FCC Daily Digest, Web site, and Audio Visual Center.

The Office of Strategic Planning & Policy Analysis (OSP) identifies policy objectives for the agency and monitors the state of the communications industry to identify trends, issues and overall industry health.

The Enforcement Bureau enforces the Communications Act. This includes the FCC rules, orders and terms, consumer protection, maintaining local competition, insuring public safety and homeland security and verifying compliance with the conditions of station authorizations.

Although the technical standards established by the various DTV organizations are voluntary, those standards (in whole or part) that are adopted as FCC rules, are binding as law. Any requirement stated as "shall" in a standard, when adopted as an FCC rule, must be implemented or adhered to. Failure to comply can result in a warning, a fine, loss of license or criminal proceedings.

The FCC Rulemaking Process

FCC Rules and Regulations are contained in the Code of Federal Regulations, Title 47. DTV rules are in Section 73.682 (d). With the adoption of the ATSC A/52 and A/53 standards, the FCC exerted its control of DTV terrestrial transmission by removing the ATSC video formats from its legally binding Rules and Regulations. The language excludes Table 3 (encoded/display formats), Section 5.1.2 and language referring to Table 3 in A/53B with Amendment 1 and 2.

The FCC Web site describes the steps in the rulemaking process:

Each time Congress enacts a telecommunications related law the FCC develops rules to implement the law.

- Notice of Inquiry (NOI): The Commission releases an NOI for the purpose of gathering information about a broad subject or as a means of generating ideas on a specific issue.

- Notice of Proposed Rulemaking (NPRM): An NPRM may be issued after reviewing public comments. It contains proposed changes to the Commission's rules and seeks public comment on these proposals.

- Further Notice of Proposed Rulemaking (FNPRM): After reviewing comments the FCC may also choose to issue an FNPRM regarding specific issues raised in comments. The FNPRM provides an opportunity for further public comments.

- Report and Order (R&O): After considering comments to a Notice of Proposed Rulemaking (or Further Notice of Proposed Rulemaking), the FCC issues a Report and Order. The R&O may develop new rules, amend existing rules or make a decision not to do so.

- Petition for Reconsideration: Parties not satisfied with the way an issue is resolved in the R&O, can file a Petition for Reconsideration within 30 days from the date the R&O appears in the Federal Register.

- Memorandum Opinion and Order (MO&O): In response to the Petition for Reconsideration, the FCC may issue a Memorandum Opinion and Order (MO&O) or an Order on Reconsideration amending the new rules or stating that the rules will not be changed.

Congress Enacts DTV Transition Legislation

Few of Congress's actions regarding telecommunications regulation have ever had the impact that Title III of the Deficit Reduction Act of 2005 will have. This is the Digital

Television Transition and Public Safety Act of 2005 (S. 1932/Public Law 109-171, February 8, 2006). The bill passed by the slim margin of 217 to 215 in the House. In the Senate, it was 52 to 47.

On February 17, 2009, NTSC terrestrial transmission will cease. Television broadcasters must relinquish their analog spectrum in the 700 MHz band. February 18, 2009 will be the first day of all-digital OTA broadcasting.

How hard is hard?

At the close of the C-Span broadcast of Congressional hearings, elected officials could be overheard commenting that they would not be surprised if in two years they all got together again to postpone the analog turnoff date.

The DTV transition legislation enables the government and all broadcast industry stakeholders—consumers, broadcasters, cable and satellite operators, manufacturers, and retailers—to prepare for the end of analog broadcasting. It also allows companies that have purchased spectrum during the FCC auctions to form definite business plans to exploit their investments.

Spectrum Auctions and Second Channel

To enable the simulcast of NTSC and DTV until the transition to digital is complete, each broadcaster was granted a second 6 MHz channel. The allocation attempts to maintain the present analog coverage footprint when a station completes its transition to full power DTV transmission capability.

A total of 108 MHz of spectrum will be recovered from analog broadcasting. 24 MHz is allocated for public safety uses. 84 MHz is allocated for advanced wireless services. Spectrum auctions began in 2001 and 60 MHz of this has yet to be auctioned. The DTV transition bill requires the FCC to begin auction of the remaining spectrum by January 28, 2006 and be completed by 2009. With a hard turn-off date for NTSC, broadcasters must plan for the cessation of their analog transmission infrastructure.

Transition Programs

The legislation gives the Department of Commerce's (DOC) National Telecommunications and Information Administration (NTIA) borrowing power to begin some programs in Fiscal Year 2007. Funding for other programs will not be available until after the spectrum is auctioned in 2008. The bill also sets specific dates for the release of funds for each program.

A fund has been created to hold proceeds from the auction of returned spectrum. On September 30, 2009, $7.363 billion will be transferred into the general Treasury fund.

Programs authorized to begin in Fiscal Year 2007 include:

- Digital-to-Analog Converter Box Assistance
- Public Safety Interoperable Communications
- NYC 9/11 Digital Transition
- Low Power Television and Translator Digital-to-Analog Conversion

Programs authorized to begin after auction proceeds are available after June 30, 2008, include:

- Low Power Television and Translator Upgrade
- National Alert and Tsunami Warning Program
- Enhance 911

Digital to Analog Converter Box Assistance

To ease the transition, the NTIA has been authorized to administer a digital-to-analog converter box assistance program. The program will provide $40 coupons to consumers to use toward the purchase of digital-to-analog converter boxes. There is a limit of two vouchers per household. $990 million is allocated to the program and is to be used solely for vouchers. The amount of available funds can be increased to $1.5 billion if necessary.

Development of prototype D-to-A boxes was funded by the NAB and MSTV, and the first models were publicly demonstrated at NAB 2006. In comment to the NTIA about coupon eligibility criteria for DTV to NTSC adapter boxes, CEA, MSTV, and NAB submitted a filing outlining performance requirements that were somewhat more demanding than those in the ATSC Recommended Practice (A/74).

Low Power Television and Translator Digital-to-Analog Conversion

Low power TV licensees fall under separate rules from full power stations. Transitioning to digital will entail a "flash-cut" turn-off of analog service and immediate initiation of digital broadcasts. Funds are being provided to help these small stations.

National Alert and Tsunami Warning Program

A national alert and tsunami warning program will be funded with $156 million distributed from fiscal year 2007 through 2012. The goal is to establish an "all hazards" alert and warning system. Although not mandated by law, the program seeks to implement multimedia capabilities on cell phones, PCs, satellite radios and other emerging technologies.

Public Safety Interoperable Communications

Interoperability of first responder communication systems will receive $1 billion.

ENHANCE 911

Funding of $43.5 million in grants is available to implement the ENHANCE 911 Act of 2004. The NTIA and USDOT have the authority to coordinate the efforts of federal, state and local emergency and safety systems, organizations and equipment vendors in developing and implementing a cell phone alert system. E-911 mobile and cellular phones will be able to receive emergency calls and enable identifying the caller's geographic location.

NYC 9/11 Digital Transition

Part of the motive to regain analog spectrum is to use it for emergency communications. New York City will be assisted with interim broadcast facilities until the Freedom Tower is completed.

The FCC and DTV

The FCC has been and will continue to be a major force in the development, rollout and future of HD and DTV. Their oversight guided the DTV transmission standardization process that culminated in the Grand Alliance prototype and ATSC standard. The FCC's actions will define business models and technical parameters for DTV in the future.

During the development of a standard, determining the amount of interference into existing NTSC channels was an important test. In fact, digital transmission of television signals was the only method of transmission that could meet this FCC requirement. So digital HDTV wasn't just better than analog, it was the only way HD could be distributed nationally over the air.

Required Features

FCC inclusion of standards in the Rules and Regulations give DTV standards the backing of law. Broadcasters are required to comply with technical specifications. Failure to do so can bring fines and problems with license renewals.

First and foremost, power, modulation depth, area coverage contour and other transmission characteristics must be adhered to. Preventing interference between DTV and other over the air transmissions is a fundamental FCC responsibility.

The FCC now requires both terrestrial broadcasters and cable systems to carry PSIP-compliant information. In fact, if a broadcaster supplies PSIP information, the FCC requires that a cable operator pass certain parts of this PSIP information unaltered.

Other DTV services that must be supported include:

- Closed Captions carried in transport streams. Presence alerts must be carried in PSIP data tables when the broadcaster sends captions

- Emergency Alert System messages must be relayed by DTV stations

- Ratings information via descriptors with the parental advisory (V-Chip) data

Compliance with the rules can be required down to the granularity of millisecond data repetition intervals, data format, content, location in the stream and many other specifications in Title 47.

Retransmission Consent

Carriage of local terrestrial broadcasters by cable networks has always been an area of contention. Should carriage be mandatory and should cable broadcasters receive remuneration for the "use" of their signal?

With DTV multicast, the complexity of the must-carry issue increases. As opposed to analog transmission, where one program always occupies the whole 6 MHz spectrum, a DTV MPEG-2 transport stream can deliver varying numbers of programs and data services. One HD program may occupy nearly the entire 19.39 Mbps transport stream capacity. Some HD programs, especially those that do not contain large amounts of action and use modern encoders may only use half the bit rate. SD programs generally use between 2 and 6 Mbps.

Bandwidth is a limited resource in cable systems. Distribution of content to headends using satellites further complicates the situation because there are a fixed number of transponder channels, limiting how much data can be handled. These factors have impacted the rollout of HD on cable systems and prompted rate shaping and statistical multiplexing techniques to reduce and manage data volume with respect to system bandwidth limits.

Multi-casting a number of services by a terrestrial broadcaster has prompted the argument that cable operators should only be required to carry a station's primary service. This would be either the HD program or main SD program in a multi-cast. Broadcasters argue that the MSO should be required to carry the complete bitstream up to 19.39 Mbps, as two such streams can be sent using 256 QAM in the same frequency band as one NTSC channel, resulting in half the number of channels used for broadcast signals in the long term.

Analog Shutdown

Broadcasters cannot simply turn off their analog transmitters. They must petition the FCC for permission to do so. The first was granted in 2002, and as 2008 approaches, the number of petitions for analog shutdown is increasing

Berlin, Germany, shut down its analog service in August 2003. The following is excerpted from the GAO report "Telecommunications: German DTV Transition Differs from U.S. Transition in Many Respects, but Certain Key Challenges Are Similar" GAO-04-926T, July 21, 2004.

- The German television market is characterized by a central role of public broadcasting and is regulated largely at the state level.

- Although the federal government establishes general objectives for the telecommunications sector and manages allocations of the German radio frequency spectrum, 15 media authorities organize and regulate broadcasting services within their areas of authority.

- Only five to seven percent of German households rely on terrestrial television.

- Germany is implementing the transition within specified "islands," which are typically larger metropolitan areas, because officials thought that a nationwide DTV transition would be too big to manage at one time.

- German DTV transition focuses exclusively on terrestrial television, not cable and satellite television.

CONTINUED ▶

CONTINUED ▶

- The Media Authority in Berlin specified other components of the DTV transition for the Berlin area, including a short (10-month) simulcast period, financial and non-financial support provided to private broadcasters, subsidies provided to low-income households and an extensive consumer education effort.

Return of their analog channel actually may be a better financial scenario for broadcasters than maintaining two transmitter infrastructures. Power savings alone may produce a substantial reduction in operating expenses. In addition, maintenance costs will be reduced as analog equipment is retired and support personnel will be available for assignment to other tasks.

Transition and Consumer Education

Some have argued that the FCC has not been active enough in communicating to consumers that when analog TV goes off the air in 2009, OTA reception will cease. If OTA is one's only means of receiving TV broadcasts, a new TV or converter box will be necessary to receive and decode DTV.

Provisions are included in the DTV transition bill for allocating funds for consumer education and the purchase of digital-to-analog converter boxes so DTV transmissions can be viewed on an analog TV. This assuaged concerns that precipitated the 85 percent DTV penetration requirement for analog shutdown, in effect prior to the passage of this bill.

Technology

Broadcasting is no longer just about broadcasting. Getting content out to as many consumers over as many channels as possible to every device anywhere for consumption at any time is the new mantra: 24/7 engagement over 360 degree delivery.

This necessitates new infrastructure design philosophies. Efficient creation, assembly and distribution must be cost-effective and get content to air quickly.

Enhanced and Interactive DTV

In the not too distant future, TVs and PCs might no longer be distinct devices, with the possible exception of use in business or education. ATSC transport stream data standards are the key to a future where media networks and presentation devices are invisibly integrated.

Targeted advertising, commercial-on-demand, additional information, and other forms of eTV and iTV will also open new revenue generating opportunities

By 2009, the majority of viewers will be Internet-savvy to say the least. In fact, by then a large number of viewers may get their TV over a broadband connection.

Multicast

The ability to broadcast more than one program over a channel can open numerous revenue opportunities. Today the capability to broadcast one HD and one SD program in an MPEG transport stream is realizable. In the future, as compression encoders improve, the possibility of fitting multiple HD programs into a transport stream will be possible.

Multi-platform

Broadcasting is no longer one-dimensional, OTA transmission. Every broadcaster has a Web site. As compression becomes more efficient, channel bandwidth higher and PCs more powerful, broadcast quality video, even HDTV, may find its principle delivery channel over the Internet.

Yet OTA DTV has advantages over other distribution channels. It is everywhere. Mobile TV is possible. Full bandwidth, 19.39 Mbps transport stream delivery will facilitate full resolution at high bit rates of difficult material to be delivered to an audience without manipulation (transcoding, rate shaping or statistical multiplexing).

Wireless and Mobile DTV

Efforts are in progress to deliver broadcast quality video and audio to wireless devices such as cell phones and PDAs. Obstacles to deployment are copyright enforcement and the size of the viewing screen.

A step towards mobile DTV has been taken by the PC industry. Laptops and notebooks can be purchased with or fitted with external USB ATSC tuners.

With DVD players factory- or customer-installed in many automobiles, the next step will be to install mobile DTV tuners. Engineering efforts are underway to solve the technical challenges inherent in design of a robust system.

Consumers and DTV Availability

The catch-22 scenario that has plagued the DTV transition for so long—while content production, distribution and consumption were locked in a stalemate—has been broken. ATSC digital tuners were required in all TVs greater than 13″ as of January 1, 2007. Some cable systems agreed to carry HDTV services in 2002, and the number of HD services available over cable continues to grow yearly. Direct-to-home satellite service providers have also followed suit and offer increasing amounts of HD content.

By many accounts, 30 percent of U.S. households will have a DTV by the end of 2006. Prices are dropping but are still a concern. Flat-panel LCD HDTV displays with a diagonal of 26″ are beginning to be available at prices below $1,000.

Most homes have more than one TV. At these 2006 price points, it will be very expensive to replace them all with DTVs. And no one wants to pay a monthly fee for cable or satellite multiple set installations.

The confusion over HD-ready, ATSC, cable-ready and other certification logos persists among consumers. Installation of digital consumer electronics and DTVs requires expertise that is often beyond the capabilities of the average consumer. This has given rise to a growing home media system installation industry. Many new homes are being constructed with media distribution cabling in the framing and often with a room dedicated to a home theatre.

This accentuates the need for home digital networks, where content is easily transferred to and from any device in the house for presentation and consumption. Consumer device interconnections transfer uncompressed video and create a bandwidth issue. Implementation of various audio modes—optical, digital and analog—further complicates matters. The emerging High Definition Multimedia Interface (HDMI) is working to solve the interconnection problem with plug-and-play capability. To the delight of the Motion Picture Association of America, the inclusion of High-bandwidth Digital Content Protection (HDCP) is expected to adequately police unauthorized transfer, copying and presentation.

However, this increases the possibility that the enforcement of copyrights may impede viewing. Problems with DVI-D and HDMI implementation of HDCP could sour consumers on DTV or result in a less than optimum media experience. This has also plagued early CableCard implementations in digital cable-ready DTV sets.

Some broadcast industry analysts report that even though an HDTV set has been purchased, many consumers do not actually watch HD programming. Instead, the NTSC simulcast is viewed. In fact, many people are still unaware that analog TV will go off the air early in 2009. The education of the consumer about high definition and DTV could stand a lot more effort.

With a content availability overload, the consumer is now in control of their entertainment experience. Just channel surf until you find something you like or use the DVR to time shift favorite shows.

But finding desired content can be difficult. The challenge is for broadcasters to make sure their target audiences know that their content is available. Search and recommender system will be indispensable.

Metadata is the key. For content creators and through the broadcast chain, persistence of content descriptive metadata is required. BOC infrastructures will have to address this in their design, as will home media networks.

Global Transitions

Japan may have beat the U.S. to air with (analog) HDTV, and Europe may have dismissed HDTV as something no one will want, but today both the Far East and Europe, as well as the rest of the globe, is transitioning to HDTV and digital broadcasting.

The International Telecommunications Union recommends that broadcast companies worldwide switch off analog broadcast programming by 2010.

Japan is targeting a hard analog HD shut off date in 2011. Korean broadcasting has similar plans and time table and in the meantime has forged ahead with iTV implementations.

China has adopted a DTV standard, known as Digital Media Broadcasting Terrestrial (DMB-T). Analog shut-down is planned for 2015.

European nations have plans to upgrade DTV to HDTV. The EBU has recommended 720p as the preferred format. HD broadcasts in Germany, Belgium, France and the United Kingdom of the 2006 World Cup were a watershed moment in the global transition to HDTV.

The Malaysian government planned to begin to shut down all analog television services in 2008 and be all-digital by 2015.

The Australian government is requiring digital broadcasting for all stations by 2012.

For broadcasters everywhere, digital offers the ability for simplified global distribution of content. This can facilitate the opportunity for anyone to enjoy content everywhere at any time. In a sense, the original NHK intent of developing a global HDTV production standard has come to fruition.

What Will Tomorrow Bring?

As broadcasting transitions into the age of HDTV and digital broadcasting, the engineering language of mathematics and the study of human psycho-sensory perception have been integrated with data reduction algorithmic methods in the development of HDTV system specifications. Adoption of these specifications as standards has consummated the marriage of broadcast engineering and information technology and spawned a new technical disciple: media systems engineering.

Diverse standards bodies now are working together in development and implementation of media technologies. Compliance with standards insures compliance with FCC rules. It also helps to insure system interoperability.

In a tapeless environment, metadata is of critical importance. If you can't locate content, you can't use it. Hence, development and standardization of metadata methodologies and practices are a major focus of work in the broadcast engineering community.

The transition is also about consumers buying new DTV receivers. It is a tremendous opportunity for the consumer electronics industry.

Copy protection will also transition to an all-digital universe and in 2009 the "analog hole" will be shutdown. Failure for an HDMI device to establish its right to content will result in either reducing picture resolution or turning off the analog outputs of a content delivery device.

The distinction between television and personal computers is dissolving.

Summary

- February 18, 2009, is the first day of all digital broadcasting in the U.S.

- Platform-agnostic media interoperability has been made possible by the conversion of content to digital.

- The need to learn about new technologies and how they enable new business models and creativity will always be present.

- No one has found the answer, but the one who does will reap the rewards of the transition.

Index